Pathways

Pathways

Charting a Course for
Professional Learning

Marjorie Larner

HEINEMANN
Portsmouth, NH

Heinemann
A division of Reed Elsevier Inc.
361 Hanover Street
Portsmouth, NH 03801–3912
www.heinemann.com

Offices and agents throughout the world

The author and publisher wish to thank those who have generously given
permission to reprint borrowed material:

Figure 6–1: Asset Map reprinted with permission from Public Education
and Business Coalition. Copyright © 1998 by PEBC.

Library of Congress Cataloging-in-Publication Data
Larner, Marjorie.
  Pathways : charting a course for professional learning / Marjorie Larner.
    p. cm.
  Includes bibliographical references.
  ISBN 0-325-00624-5
  1. Teachers—In-service training. 2. Effective teaching. 3. School
improvement programs. I. Title.
  LB1731.L38 2004
  370'.71'5—dc22   2003018828

Editor: Danny Miller
Production: Elizabeth Valway
Cover design: Jenny Jensen Greenleaf
Cover photo: Samantha Bennett
On the cover (from left to right): Lynn Reynolds, Sangita Patel, Tim Reyes, and
Marlecia Jenkins from Prairie Middle School, Cherry Creek School District,
Aurora, Colorado
Composition: Argosy
Manufacturing: Steve Bernier

Printed in the United States of America on acid-free paper
08 07 06 05 04 VP 1 2 3 4 5

To the children and adults who spend their days in school.

Contents

Foreword

Recently a colleague confided that her district had invited her to become a literacy coach for teachers in three elementary schools. I expressed my delight, congratulated her, and asked about the teachers with whom she might be working. She responded to my enthusiasm with a somewhat heavy heart, and I could see she felt conflicted about the new responsibilities. "I know it's a great opportunity," she began. Then she shook her head. "I'm just not sure I can pull it off. I do what I do in my own classroom without thinking too much about it, and I don't have any idea how to help other teachers improve their practice. Plus, I just can't bear to stop teaching."

School districts are increasingly aware of and acting on research suggesting that classroom-based coaching is a highly effective way for teachers to better align their practices with current learning research. Fine teachers across the country are being invited to leave their classrooms, at least part of the time, to serve as staff developers for their colleagues. District policy makers understand that in order to effect lasting improvements in teaching and learning, teachers need opportunities to experiment with new practices and that these experiments are best accomplished with a coach at every teacher's side.

But how should school districts support these coaches or staff developers? What types of knowledge and training will best serve teachers making the transition to staff development positions? What do staff developers need to understand about adult learning in order to coach effectively? How much theory does a coach need to know in the content area on which he or she will focus? And perhaps the most basic and important question: is a good teacher automatically a good coach?

My colleague had reservations about her ability to coach and regarded her potential career move as a departure from teaching. When she inquired about planned training and support for the newly named literacy coaches, she found that nothing much had been planned or budgeted for. After all, weren't *they* supposed to provide the support? Suddenly, the classroom in which she taught seemed appealingly comfortable and safe, and the teachers in her district lost the opportunity to learn from one of the finest of their number.

I have been privileged to work in staff development for over seventeen years and have watched the field evolve as a result of a few brave souls who were willing just to get out there and work side by side with colleagues without support from their school districts and without knowing exactly *how* to support teachers' learning and growth. Unfortunately for the teachers with whom I worked, I had little opportunity to learn *how* to coach. I traipsed into schools, sat down with teachers, and told them we were going to experiment together, see how the children reacted, and revise our practices accordingly.

I, too, was concerned about leaving the classroom, and on more than one occasion resolved to return—only to be reminded by my superintendent that I *was* teaching, just in a different form: I was teaching teachers. He was absolutely right. Working with colleagues is teaching of the most potent and highly developed kind. Teaching a group of children while simultaneously thinking aloud to the observing adults about how and why one is making certain decisions requires not only superb teaching skills but also a range of additional professional development strategies.

The bad news is that most school districts are still not prepared to provide the kind of training and support that coaches need and deserve. The great news is that we have books like *Pathways: Charting a Course for Professional Learning* to help fill the void. In this extraordinary volume, Marjorie Larner responds to the question I am perhaps asked more than any other: *What do I need to know in order to provide meaningful pro-*

fessional learning opportunities to colleagues? In doing so, she shows us how we can create and capitalize on a culture of continuous learning in our schools. Given the move toward more school-based professional learning in this country, the timing for this important book could not be better.

A former teacher and principal turned staff developer, Marjorie has seen professional learning from a variety of angles, all of which permit her to illuminate the hazy, oblique world of adult learning in schools. *Pathways* offers extremely practical sets of questions and lists to guide the planning and implementing of effective, school-based professional learning. It is a book for teachers, teacher leaders, and principals—for professionals who care so much about children's learning, they understand the critical need for high-quality adult learning opportunities.

But it is Marjorie's voice in this fine book that delights me most. Throughout it is as if she is sitting in the room with me, helping me be thoughtful and deliberate as I plan for teachers' learning—helping me avoid the pitfalls of omission to which I'm all too prone. Lyrically and gently, she prods me to *learn* from the voices of dissenters, capitalize on known successes, and take the time to build the necessary structures rather than stumble into poorly planned workshops and demonstrations. She acknowledges my sense of urgency that the work must be done quickly and well if children are to have more equitable access to excellent teaching, but she also cautions me that change takes time and that there are signs of change that mark the path.

I especially appreciate the way Marjorie capitalizes on something we teachers, at least instinctively, understand—just as there is a gradual release of responsibility from teacher to children when a new and complex concept is being learned, so there must be a gradual release of responsibility from colleague to colleague in professional venues. This makes so much sense, but I can't count the number of times I've tried to circumvent it in the mistaken belief that teachers can use new strategies without fully understanding and supporting them.

In fact, Marjorie makes the point that those colleagues who seem intransigent may in fact be exercising strong professional judgment—not jumping on every bandwagon without fully knowing how it will impact their students.

Marjorie's understanding of professional relationships and the impact of those relationships on school culture is nothing short of astounding. Using myriad examples from elementary and secondary schools, she makes clear how absolutely essential it is to engage all members of a school community but goes much further to suggest a wide spectrum of ways in which we can bring many voices to the table. Instead of talking in generalities and abstractions, she takes us into the lives of dozens of teachers and staff developers who have benefited from her work in the Denver area. Their (occasionally hilarious) experiences are so similar to our own, we have to wonder whether they were in the room with us!

I know few people in the country who could have written this book as wisely or as well. I can't help wondering whether my colleague who chose to remain in the classroom might have made a different decision if I had had this book to recommend to her. Had she read these perspectives on schooling and professional learning, informed as they are by Marjorie's diverse experience, she might have agreed that her considerable skills as a teacher might find a new, very compatible home in coaching her colleagues.

In any event, we now are fortunate to have *Pathways*, a gem of a book in which Marjorie is willing to sit beside us, help us consider the subtleties and nuances of teachers' learning, and regale us along the way with stories from her own journey. Somehow, knowing that someone else has passed this way before makes our own journey more hopeful, makes the pathway we have chosen more understandable.

Ellin Oliver Keene

Acknowledgments

I always imagined writing a book in collaboration, so when I found myself writing alone, I wondered how I would do it. As it turned out, I was rarely on my own. Family, colleagues, and friends have been generous with their time and expertise. While this book is filtered through the lens of my experiences and beliefs, it has been a collaboration with many others, which leads to a long list of people to acknowledge.

My dear friend, Sandy Stollery, gave hours and days of her time to help me in every aspect of writing this book. When I continued to chafe at writing a book alone and still found myself in that position, Sandy stepped in as a partner to talk with about the big concepts as well as each minute detail. Who else would stare at the computer with me for days going through line after line and fretting over each word? In truth, Sandy, you are in every word and thought of this book.

And thanks to Vic Belba for your technical support and your sweet patience with all the time Sandy gave to this effort.

My sister, Judith Larner Lowry, has always paved the way and then held out a hand to help me follow. Thank you for cutting through the distractions to point out the next step, especially when it was hard to take. I hear your beautiful writer's voice beckoning me to strive for the best I can do.

My brother, Bernard Larner, makes sure I keep a toe in practicality so that I can survive while trying to accomplish my dreams. Thank you for bringing that same sensibility to your comments on my writing. And thank you for always being there for me in these last years.

The family legacy conveyed to me by my late parents, Sara and Irv Larner, is that strain of idealism that leads me to keep trying to save the world. I watched my aunts, uncles, and cousins set an example for me to follow. From my earliest memories, Deborah Meier inspired me to see what is right and live it.

As a young teacher, I was profoundly influenced by my ten years with The Prospect School, a small independent school in North Bennington, Vermont. Although no longer a school for children, it still maintains an archive of children's work and an active cadre of continuing scholar-educators. I thank Patricia F. Carini for sharing her brilliant intellect and understanding in such a way that I could see through the ordinary doors to amazing possibilities for human beings.

Many friends and colleagues stepped in at crucial moments to help me take the next leap. Without Sam Bennett and her fine capacity for organizing, I'd probably still be working on early drafts. Thank you for wading through it all to help me find the spark and sense in my writing and in our work together. Fran Jenner brought her gentle yet piercing perspective to an early reading that pointed the way to what was important. Fran, you are a master at finding the right encouraging word to help a person continue. I thank Joy Hood, who insisted she loved my writing, helped me remember the point of what I was doing at every step, and often shared the burden and made me laugh, calling me at odd times with an idea to help clarify or focus my circular thoughts. Joy, you are the best. All along the way Ann Goudvis listened and reassured me that I could do this. Anne, you have given me ground to stand on the many times I was sure I was lost in my own wandering thoughts about our work.

I thank the Boulder Valley middle level principals cohort— Ellen Miller-Brown, Scott Winston, Adam Fels, Janice Christie, Joni Beall, Candy Hyatt, Alice Lindemann—for letting me be the facilitator of your meetings. You have taught me about heroism in our jobs and given me inspiration, hope, and much new knowledge.

Ellin Oliver Keene has worked hard to help us become great teachers, readers, and writers. Ellin, I thank you for your guiding and encouraging words after reading early pages that set me on a more definite course. Whenever I hit points where I could not find my writer's voice, I would read a page in *Mosaic of Thought*, and the images and real stories would start flooding my mind and I could write again.

To the adults and children at Foster Elementary School, who forever changed my view of what we can achieve, thank you for your patience and willingness to share your stories and classrooms with me.

I continue to share the joy of wondering with Carrie Symons and Susan McIver. I know that with opportunities to watch you both teaching, I will always find new ideas and insights about learning.

I thank every teacher and student along the way and especially my friends at Aspen Creek K–8, University Hill Elementary School, Base Line Middle School and School for the Arts, Casey Middle School, Witt Elementary School, Heatherwood Elementary School, and Prairie Middle School.

I offer gratitude to everyone at PEBC for genuine support of adults and children in schools. I am thankful to work with other people who believe in our own capacities and in each child's capacity to read, write, and think with passion and enthusiasm. I'm grateful for the opportunities to watch the practice of Debbie Miller, Cris Tovani, and Carole Quinby—teachers who are living proof that everything we hope for in the classroom is possible. Stephanie Harvey and Chryse Hutchins provided a high standard for scholarship in our profession that has deepened the quality of work for all of us.

My friends—Marthe Gold, Arleen LaBella, Catherine Rubin, Janice Wall, Sue Pisano, William Sleator, and Nancy Greystone—listened, soothed my worries, and celebrated my triumphs. Beth Record, thank you for being here.

I have been grateful to work with production editor, Elizabeth Valway. Thank you for your skill, patience, and calm voice that confidently carried the book through each stage.

To Danny Miller, without whom I would never have even begun, much less completed, this book. Your confidence and your great mind, not to mention your sense of humor, lured me to continue and strive for wonderful writing. I appreciate the many times you reminded me why I was doing this, who it was for, and why you thought it had value.

In my heart while writing this book, I held my three sons, Cass, Josh, and Alex Epstein, who have brought the experience of school life—both the joys and the sorrows—home to me in sometimes excruciatingly poignant ways. My great advisors, always helping me see what I don't know and where I need to improve, thank you for your inspiration and patience with my journey as a writer and the joy you bring me as a mother watching you grow.

Introduction

Life is a path you beat while you walk it.

—Anthony Marcado

"So what do you suggest we do?" The principal leaned across her desk in the dimly lit office while I sat with a notebook in my lap, pen poised to take notes on our planning session for my professional development work with the teachers in her building. Five teachers and a district literacy coach—the school's leadership team—awaited my response. A general goal of increased instructional efficacy and, more pointedly, increased test scores, floated in the air around us. We had only a few minutes left in this meeting to sketch out a meaningful plan for professional learning attached to specific goals for student learning. They wanted a quick and clear plan of action. Which aspect of instruction, of student need, of school culture would we address first?

Images came to mind of particular teachers who transformed their teaching, and whole faculties who embraced a common effort leading to ongoing improvement. I noted in them a consistent commitment to concrete and specific structures and activities within a context of understanding, belief, and a philosophy that infused their action with meaning and worth.

Drawing on research and my own experience, I offered my synthesis of the necessary components of school change:

- Consensus in regard to underlying beliefs and understandings about teaching and learning that inform the school's goals

- An agreed-upon instructional model grounded in research and experience
- Recognition of the history and dynamics in the school culture
- An articulated framework for professional study that is clear, developmental, and based on sound principles of teaching and learning
- A plan to sustain a long-term commitment

What I have seen is not a brief or simple process, but rather a rich and complex constellation of ideas, steps, and structures. Nor is it an effort that lasts just two years, or even five years, but rather it is an ongoing effort that continues as long as a person is teaching. If we agreed to work together, I said, these components would provide the road map for professional learning that would improve instruction in their school.

I promised the team that, above all, I would try to work with the particular needs, strengths, and goals of the individual adults in the school, just as I work with each child in a classroom. I explained why they would want to plan for a variety of entry points, including ways they could learn from each other as well as the role that outside consultants might play. I described my strategic and interactive approach to instruction for learners of all ages.

While their plan would be drawn from the experiences of other school communities, we would chart their first steps and long-term course to fit their particular community and unique culture. So I began the conversation by asking them to describe their school to me. I listened carefully as they began to talk about teaching and learning in the context of the needs of their students, district support and constraints, and the richness and challenges of a diverse population. They reported data on test scores, staff turnover and mobility, absenteeism, suspension, and graduation rates. They shared their dreams of what they would like to see the school become.

I listened for the team's underlying assumptions and expectations about the possibilities for the teachers and students that would either extend or limit their reach. Beneath the spoken conversation were other, implicit questions that would determine the first step we would take. How much can we improve the teaching in our school? Can teachers who are considered ineffective become effective? Can the already good ones become great? Can the great become greater? Can we improve learning for students who are struggling? How long before we will see results for student learning? How will we know we are making progress?

These questions, and the answers I've heard over the years, echoed in my mind. Joy Hood, former principal and current coach and mentor, often reminds me, "If they knew a better way, they would do it." If we believe that, then we don't blame ourselves, but we look at how to find a better way. I appreciate the people who have the personality and instinct to inspire students because they know how to form relationships and make information engaging. We have all been in schools where teachers light up the eyes and minds of their students. And, we are all aware of the struggles inherent in the effort to meet the learning needs of every person.

Fran Jenner, a fellow staff developer, says that our first job is to help each person find at least one of their strengths as a place to begin. That strength could lie in a teacher's appreciation for her students or a determination to help them succeed. It could be a belief in the power of instruction or a personal love of learning.

I have seen people, and whole school communities, find their better way when neither they, nor anyone else, believed it was possible. Mary Ross, a former Title One teacher at Foster Elementary School in Arvada, Colorado, told me that her school's staff developers, Ellin Keene and Stephanie Harvey, "told us we were wonderful. We thought we were not as good as the teachers in the more affluent schools because our test scores were low. They told us we were smart and we started to believe them."

A teacher's belief rests in the capacity for each person—teacher and student—to learn and grow. Joy has often reminded me, "You have to look in the right places." I have come to agree with her, because every day spent in a school supplies stories that support this point of view; the teacher who discovered a previously unrealized love of writing while transforming her classroom of jaded seventh-grade students into a community of hardworking, passionate, and skillful writers; the zealous third-grade teacher who learned how to structure his up-to-then chaotic class so that every child completed an organized creative research project; an entire eighth-grade class of widely diverse students who surprised everyone when they all scored in the "proficient" category on the state standardized test; and the revitalized middle school faculty who started off as adversaries of their students, then became advocates and guides for their students' learning by looking deeply at their own learning and practice, identifying effective strategies and skills, and beginning to see and believe in the strengths, desires, and great potential of everyone in the school.

So I often tell principals, "Don't give up on anyone yet. You never know who might make the greatest leaps." They frequently laugh in recognition of a comment they make to teachers when discussing challenging students.

In a story of Thomas Edison, who reportedly made 2,000 attempts to invent the lightbulb before it worked, a young journalist asked him, "How did it feel to fail 2,000 times?" Thomas Edison reportedly replied, "Young man, I never failed. It was a 2,000-step process."

This book is a synthesis of the many steps I have seen lead to improved instruction for students. It is intended to provide a guide for teachers, coaches, and principals, ideally working collaboratively, to chart their own course for their own school's improvement.

In witnessing the varied pathways that individuals and school communities have followed, I have always seen a consistent commitment to specific structures and activities within a context of articulated understanding and beliefs about teaching and learning. With that awareness, I have tried to weave these dual approaches throughout the book—offering the actual examples of activities and structures as well as the thinking and rationale behind them—in a meaningful, rather than rote, way. Guiding questions open each chapter and provide a tool for readers to make connections and applications to their own experience.

Setting our sights on new destinations, we are like Dorothy taking her first steps on the yellow brick road to the Emerald City. At first she walks a very tight spiral, and seems to be getting nowhere. Actually, she is getting focused and ready to move forward, with the destination firmly fixed in her mind. The first three chapters are that circling—getting oriented in the right direction toward clear goals. Chapters 4 through 6 offer the specific activities and steps to move forward—concrete frameworks for professional learning and structures to assess what is producing desired results in order to sustain a long-term commitment. In Chapter 7, the story of one elementary school community, from the beginning of their change efforts to the years of sustaining growth, provides one possible picture of how all the pieces can be pulled together. The last chapter addresses the relationship of school professionals to the larger world context and the importance and possibilities of an influential voice in that realm. There are a number of figures throughout the book that can be photocopied for classroom use. They are also available in a larger format on the Heinemann website, *heinemann.com*.

While writing this book, one image lingered in my mind from a moment after that meeting with the principal and leadership team many years ago. On my way out of the office, after an intense two hours immersed in the big picture of the school culture and the team's efforts to increase student learning, I passed two teachers standing just outside the office door, reading a student's story together. They commented on the vocabulary and spelling, wondering how they could help this particular child remember unfamiliar words. They continued talking animatedly as they moved down the hallway to the cafeteria. Their overriding worry and concern while they brainstormed struck me. Here was what really mattered. A teacher and her colleague. A student and his work. A particular, as yet unmet, need for teaching and learning. This is the driving force behind professional learning in the teaching field.

I remembered a quote from Joseph Campbell in his book, *The Hero with a Thousand Faces* (1972): "The hero shows the power of the human imagination to attempt the impossible." I have seen many heroes in schools over the years.

Pathways

Chapter 1

Underlying Beliefs
About Teaching and Learning

When it's something you care about, I think it's easier.

—Eighth-grade student

Guiding Questions

What memory of your own experience as a student stands out?
What reading lingers in your thoughts about teaching and learning?
What were you formally taught about teaching and learning?
What has experience taught you about teaching and learning?
What strategies and skills can you rely on for effective instruction?
What picture do you imagine for your students' future?
How are you and your colleagues preparing them for this future?

*E*veryone enters teaching with years of experience as a student. What we believe about how students learn is most profoundly informed by our own experience. My belief in the potential for human beings to learn is the foundation for my teaching and emerges from my own story and experiences in life—as a learner and as a teacher.

My undergraduate education courses in the early 1970s focused our attention more on how to see ourselves and realize our value as human beings, than on methods for teaching. Although we practiced filling out lesson plans for delivery of information, the main thrust was that if students felt good and confident, they would naturally soak up learning. We learned an approach but very little pedagogy.

I believe this approach arose as it became evident that our world was changing and that educational requirements would need to extend beyond traditional delivery. How this pedagogy should look was not yet apparent or visible. Those years were a time of exciting experimentation in education that mirrored the climate of other aspects of society. I see now that we focused on critical principles of building learning communities as a precursor to developing critical elements of pedagogy. We were dealing with the personal and relational aspects of culture, yet not addressing the core purpose of why we were there together—that is, student learning.

I went into teaching wildly inspired. I suspect I was less prepared than new teachers today who, in many cases, do learn effective methods of instruction. My intuition was my primary resource and that, I discovered, was not adequately developed for the awesome responsibility I would assume.

Reflective Learning: The Prospect School

I was hired to teach nine- through eleven-year-old children at The Prospect School, a small, private school of only four teachers and one hundred children in the village of North Bennington, Vermont. As a young teacher, I was profoundly influenced by this school where, I thought, education was envisioned in its simplest and richest context. The underlying beliefs that cofounder and executive director Patricia Carini articulated resonated with my deepest aspirations for education. She wrote, "In my own observations of children, I start from the context of certain assumptions about our humanness. In the first place, I assume that most people—and most children—are not pathological, although each is unique in terms of specific outlook and perceptions. I assume too that, barring drastic damage to the organism, all people—and all children—think, seek to make sense of the world, and hold in common a questioning, wondering posture" (1986). From this assumption, we continually explored how to create an environment, provide experiences, and guide learning for children and for ourselves in order to nurture the potential for thinking and making sense of the world.

When I have reminisced with friends about my time at The Prospect School, they sometimes tell me, in effect, "that was a very different time and place and we could never do that these days." With a closer look, however, the connection to today's most current understanding of best practices in teaching and learning becomes evident. Finding personal meaning, learning through inquiry, and observation and reflection of students and one's own process are just a few aspects of current best practice that has roots in the work of many teachers and researchers from those days, including the members of The Prospect School community.

With the freedom of a curriculum that emerged from students' interests, and my lack of experience, I wasn't sure what to do in the beginning. Everyone gave me suggestions for activities and projects. I tried to implement every single one of their ideas. The students and I read and wrote, made poetry books, explored numbers, and went for walks collecting specimens for scientific study. We developed sweet relationships as we explored our thoughts through poetry, singing, and group meetings. I could count on capturing the whole group's attention by telling stories. But what essential learning was occurring for these children during this time? I sincerely hoped it was what they needed.

Participating in every professional education opportunity the school offered, I joined teachers from around the country as well as my colleagues and other community members in weekly seminars and summer institutes where we explored issues in learning and careful study of students through their work. We read philosophy and literature as they applied to learning, as well as books on education. My eyes were opened to a greater dynamic, the underlying purpose of classroom life.

3

I grasped a context within which to make decisions and plans for each child as well as for the class. Without this understanding, I could implement activities with the best of intentions but had no sure chance of meeting learning goals for students. With this understanding, I could create meaningful plans for each student's progress.

Enthralled with the study of teaching and learning, I took a new job, created for someone to "float" wherever needed. Working everywhere allowed me to see each detail of the complex running of the classrooms and school. I continued to learn through inquiry and discovery—by watching students, observing our own teaching practice, and reflecting on what and how everyone was learning. Within the atmosphere of a school that saw itself as a laboratory for learning and research, I continued to develop my understanding and skill by watching, practicing, reflecting. This became my real schooling in how to be a teacher, and it foreshadowed a process that would eventually become an explicit framework for all my work as a teacher and learner.

A Culture of Thinking and Learning: Public Education and Business Coalition

When I left that isolated Vermont world in 1991 to take a job as director of a new private school in Boulder, Colorado, I was jolted into a very different, bigger world. I had a lot to learn and get used to. People had programs and books and brand names to identify how they taught. They had the advantage of published collections of creative activities with black-line masters to make copies for student practice instead of individually customizing each assignment. Teachers determined curriculum in advance so they could prepare before the school year started. The move was toward one structure for teaching everyone toward one vision of success. This was very far removed from the intimate inner relationship of one teacher and one child sitting close together during a cloudy Vermont winter morning, feeling their way along. I reveled in the eternal Colorado sunshine and certainly saw some advantages to this clear system-atized approach. It appeared more practical and recognizably productive. I was grateful for the foundation of depth, intimacy, and meaningful early experiences and I was determined to hold onto that base, yet I saw that the next step of learning would draw on a different base of research and professional literature.

In a conversation with another mother on my youngest son's first day of public school, I heard about the Public Education and Business Coalition (PEBC). PEBC was begun by a group of attorneys and educators in the 1980s, with "a vision of a local education fund designed to identify and support innovative practices in public schools, while providing systemic change from outside the system" (Keene and Zimmermann 1997). The first staff developers began working in classrooms with teachers, intensively exploring how to apply current research findings to effective literacy instruction. Staff developers and participating teachers began to focus on the proficient reader research (or "what good readers do") conducted by P. David Pearson, Jan Dole, and others. These studies determined that good readers think and interact with the text in ways that could be explicitly identified as strategies to construct meaning and understanding: activating prior knowledge, asking questions, determining importance, creating imagery, making inferences, and synthesizing. Proficient readers also monitor their comprehension and use fix-up strategies when they lose their way. With the identification of these strategies, everyone could be let in on the mystery of how to think, understand, and learn.

An Explicit Instructional Model

Teachers who work with PEBC report that the "gradual release of responsibility" model for teaching has been one of the most powerful changes in their practice, leading to deep thinking and lasting learning. The model articulated by Fielding and Pearson (1994) for teaching reading comprehension strategies follows a sequence of teacher modeling, guided practice, independent practice and, finally, application to real situations.

This is probably the most ancient method for teaching, to some extent lost over the years as presentation of information became more the norm. I think of countless examples of apprentices, athletes, and artists, all learning by watching masters, and slowly, as they learned the steps, taking on more of the work themselves. With the articulation of this gradual release sequence, teachers have regained a powerful instructional tool. When combined with rich and significant content, students and teachers engage in interaction and thought as a means for holding on to and applying learning.

In my earlier years in classrooms, drawing on intuition and instinct, I struggled to find ways to interest the children through my own energy or ideas. Finally I found reliable steps and strategies—a framework—to achieve the intimacy and depth through an intellectually rigorous instructional process. I learned that if I modeled skills to succeed, strategies to support thinking, and choice within structure, students wholeheartedly accepted the invitation to join me in meaningful learning in the classroom.

This type of instruction impacts the community and relationships of everyone in the school as they learn to value their own and others' thinking. Pragmatism can be balanced and integrated with ideals. In fact, this kind of collaborative learning leads to intimate relationships and a cohesive, focused culture of learners.

Beliefs About Teaching and Learning

My agenda is for students to really understand who they are and how they fit into society.

—Sangita Patel, seventh-grade social studies
teacher, Prairie Middle School

Decisions about what, why, and how to teach grow increasingly difficult in the face of all the currently promoted methods, activities, and standards for content and skill. The way a person teaches and what he teaches rests on beliefs about human capacities and purpose. What do we need to know? What do we need to be able to do? What is the potential of each person for knowing? Beliefs supported by research and experience provide a consistent guide for confident decision making.

At The Prospect School, we believed in the profound meaning that a human being finds in life, that "people—and all children—think, seek to make sense of the world, and hold in common a questioning, wondering posture" (Carini 1986, 17). At PEBC, the belief is in everyone's capacity to learn to read, write, and think. We prove this to ourselves nearly every day as we continually engage in our own learning to become better readers, writers, thinkers, and teachers. While these beliefs may be articulated and put into practice with variations, the underlying value resides in a similar worldview of human development.

As educators, we often find the studies and books that resonate with our particular experiences to validate our beliefs and provide the foundation of our teaching. Many teachers post reminders at strategic places around their classrooms. Principals post them in public areas around the school. For me, A. C. Harwood's reminder that my work as a teacher or as a staff developer begins with intimate engagement with the person keeps me on track under pressure: "The most important thing, both for parents and teachers, is to have the right feeling for a child; and this feeling can only arise out of a true understanding of all that happens in childhood" (1981). This leads me to continually seek and explore further knowledge about human development and the process of learning.

The Purpose of Education

The purpose of teaching and instruction is to bring ever more *out* of man rather than to put more into him; for that which can get *into man* we already know and possess as the property of mankind. On the other hand, what yet is to come *out* of mankind, what nature is yet to develop, that we don't yet know. (Froebel 1974)

Within the exploration of best practices in instruction, clarity and information about essential purpose and outcomes is crucial. What are we teaching for? Throughout the literature on teaching for understanding in all areas of learning, a strategic process is identified through which learners construct meaning and internalize learning by interacting—with the text, with others, and with their own thinking. In *State of the Art: Transforming Ideas for Teaching and Learning to Read* (1993), Anne P. Sweet and co-authors describe literacy instruction: "understanding meta-cognition and helping students develop tools with which to direct their own learning . . . [teachers are] key agents who ensure that each child enters the pathway to becoming a literate adult, and who guide students in their ascending journey every step of the way."

This model of teaching as guiding "students in their ascending journey every step of the way" fits within a model of learning that is remembering, applying, extending; being changed in your view and your behavior; making use of what you hear and see; and making it your own. With this view of teaching and learning, debates over phonics versus whole language, self-esteem versus high expectations, community versus individual accountability, compassion versus rigor are a distracting tangent because each element is necessary for the other. How can you achieve true self-esteem without accomplishment? How can you have a community if individuals don't take responsibility for themselves? How do you build genuine relationships without knowing each other's thinking? How can you continue to make meaning from text if you can't eventually decipher words on your own?

To anyone outside the field of education, this view might seem obvious. In practice, within the field, we are dizzied by all we must and want to do. At a principal's study group, we heard that teachers didn't feel they could slow down to ensure understanding and deep learning because they had so much district-mandated curriculum to cover. The district representative at the meeting tried to help: "You have to choose from the district curriculum notebook what is essential." She paused. "And everything in there is really good and essential."

Good and essential. Are these criteria that we can use? The time that teachers have with students in school is limited. Every minute matters. It may not be practical to use any percentage of that time exposing them to content to be remembered only in the short term. It is not even fair when we use fancy engaging activities to trick them into learning while they think they're just having fun. Many of us have a store of fantastically creative, engaging, labor-intensive lessons we have taught "that the students loved." But are they learning what is good and essential? How do we decide? And how do we make it possible? Have we created the daunting complexity of our lessons because distractions have clouded the view so we can't see what is essential?

Sangita Patel, a seventh-grade social studies teacher and chair of the social studies department at Prairie Middle School, tried to tackle this issue in an email to her social studies colleagues. She wrote, "If we are to get our students thinking deeply and making connections . . . we need to give them choice on how they want to think and what they want to determine as important. As I continue my work with staff developers, I realize that I am pushing myself beyond my comfort zone as a teacher to become an instructor of thought for my students . . . I have had to give up many activities that I loved doing, but then realized there was no true depth to them in the first place."

If we are teaching for true deep learning based on student need, we do not have to lure students into learning with teacher-intensive activities so they think they're having fun. Learning is the most fun. It makes a person feel bigger, competent, and powerful. Engagement in learning distracts from worries about what may be going on at home or with friends in the hallways. Knowledge and understanding are powerful tools that help a person live her life. Indeed, skills and knowledge can save a life.

Learning is a basic human activity—necessary for our survival in the world. Teaching is also a basic human activity—an innate desire and responsibility to prepare our children for life and survival. Arguably, the skills and knowledge needed to function in current times have become more intricate and increasingly harder to recognize. In order to penetrate this complexity, we have to locate the common threads underlying acquisition of any skill or knowledge.

Through research as well as experience and even common sense, educators are developing an understanding of learning and teaching that is not about fancy gimmicks to trick the students into learning or heavy consequences to force the students to hold onto information for tests. Nor is it only possible through the magic of a few teachers with inborn instincts or the right personalities. Rather, learning relies on activating the learner's intellect so he takes in information, mulls it around, and comes to own it. Eighth-grade language arts teacher Mary Bode tells her students she provides opportunities for them to manipulate the information to make it their own. Or as I say, teachers help students digest the information so they make it part of themselves and thus are nourished to grow with a sound foundation for more learning. When teachers help students see the value and power in their thinking and realize that thinking is actually the essential thread in the quality of their learning, problem solving, and decision making, students engage and grow.

Even without the issues of high-stakes testing, there is an undeniable urgency for children to be educated in such a way that they can become functional members of the modern society.

This urgency requires absolute clarity about the effect of every instructional opportunity. In his book, *Intellectual Character* (2002), Ron Ritchart refers to a distinction between instruction that provides opportunities for learning and instruction that is an opportunity for work or task completion. A teacher under considerable pressure to show results of her students' learning through increased test scores once said to me after I'd spent a few minutes in her classroom looking over her assignments, "Do you think I'm doing okay? Will you tell my principal I'm doing good things?" I told her, "You'd be the best judge of that. Is what you're doing working for the students? Are they completing tasks or are they learning? Are they learning what they need to be learning? It doesn't matter what I think. You know so much more about what is happening with your students' learning." This led her to slow down long enough to observe her students and identify which activities were engaging their thinking and growth and which activities required only that they go through the motions of task completion. Continuing to observe her students, she developed her own body of knowledge of appropriate and effective practice for her students' learning. Then she could begin to identify which aspects of her instructional plan to increase and which to decrease.

The Teacher's Purpose

Pressure is on teachers and schools at every level as they aim to bring each child from every background to equal achievement. As Deborah Meier writes in her book, *The Power of Their Ideas* (1995) "Schools embody the dreams we have for our children. All our children." In order to reach all our children, we need to reach all their teachers. The evidence supporting the key influence of quality teachers in school reform is so overwhelming that the National Commission on Teaching and America's Future (1996) states, "A caring, competent and qualified teacher for every child is the most important ingredient in educational reform."

What does this teacher who reaches all students do? I catch many gripes from friends and acquaintances about teachers they have known. They are so sure of what isn't working. When I ask what would be a great teacher, they often duck that question in favor of further descriptions of bad teachers. Fortunately, many people within the field have attempted to define what makes a great teacher. It is a broad and complex conception.

My view of teachers derives from all the roles I have seen fulfilled. Teachers inspire, motivate, discipline, and inform. Teachers are artists, as Thomas Moore describes in *The Reenchantment of Everyday Life* (1996), "keepers of enchantment . . . struggling to maintain contact with a universe that is alive and soaked in meaning."

When Carrie Symons, an extraordinary third-year teacher at Harrington Elementary School in Denver, Colorado, was asked how she had so quickly become a great and effective teacher, she wrote: "I realized I wanted to go into teaching after many months of soul searching and asking myself, 'What could I do every minute, every day . . . what could I be consumed with that I would love?' At that point, I didn't know how valuable my background in the performing arts would be in my teaching. I didn't realize then that teaching is the highest art form possible."

Indeed, teachers like Carrie are poets and storytellers bridging the gap between the known and the unknown. As poets, they bring the world of metaphor and meaning to us in the language they use. As storytellers, teachers ground complicated ideas in concrete terms, give them a flesh-and-blood reality, emphasize what is valued, watched, rewarded. Teachers choreograph their classrooms—the setting, the movements, the pace and the shape of it—so that students may achieve goals and move as individuals in a group. Teachers use dramatic pauses, body stance, gesture and tone of voice to hold attention and hearts, just as great dramatic performers do. Notice the way a teacher leans in to hear a child speak, pauses at the climax of the story, holds her hands as if to hold the group in her embrace.

Teachers create music in the lives of children, the quiet hum of busy engagement, the loud and quiet voices, just as musicians use sound to captivate, calm, or excite. Teachers paint pictures of our world and ourselves in it. They create "an aesthetic environment in which we can learn and grow" (Campbell, Campbell, and Dickinson 1998). Teachers must "be interested in something or someone not for one's own gain or aggrandizement but instead an interest that makes room for some other—a person, a painting, an idea (subject matter, thoughts)—to be in its own right, to appreciate and even cherish that person" (Carini 2000).

Finally, teachers show students the value of discipline, rigor, and effort. They model what it looks to be a writer, a researcher, and a scholar. They help their students gather skills so their efforts lead to meaningful results. They help them recognize accomplishments as well as what comes next. Great teachers believe in their own capacities for greatness as much as they believe in the possibilities for the children.

The School's Purpose

> Basically there's nothing that you can do that is as powerful for raising student achievement as investing in what teachers know and can do. (Darling-Hammond 1998)

The qualities that are present or lacking in teachers as a group determine the quality of the school culture, which is, necessarily, more than a building or repository for faculty and students. Jonathan Raban's account of the early prairie schools in *Bad Land: An American Romance*, provides insight into the historical role of the school in our society, "The schoolhouse was an emblem of the fact that people were here for keeps. Its foundations were dug deep enough into the prairie to hold one's own ambitious roots . . . the schoolhouse was the center of things. . . . For everyday inspiration and enlightenment, for a code of practical morality, for as much in the way of uplift as a body can reasonably stand, one could look to the schoolhouse on the hill. The building and its books stood for a creed that everyone believed in: progress;

self-improvement; a faith in the great metaphysical abstraction of America" (1996).

This is a tall order to fill and, I believe, one for which we still yearn. As a nation, we expect schools to embody multiple values, traditions, and stability. Hypothetically, public schools exist as a place for children to get all skills and knowledge they need to become functioning members of a democratic capitalist society.

Therefore, all aspects of a well-functioning school culture arise from a model for teaching and learning that builds community, responsibility, and critical-thinking and problem-solving skills. This can take us beyond some of the philosophical value-laden debates to bodies of evidence that inform decisions about teaching. The practice informed by these decisions is what makes us who we are as teachers and as school communities.

A Yearning for Growth: Learning to Teach

> Like the seeds of perennial plants, [internalized understandings] keep putting out new shoots for growth, searching for space and fertile ground, growing in sometimes unpredictable directions. (Lowry 1999)

I have asked many of the most enthusiastic teachers what it is that leads them to take risks and continually try new ways. They describe a way of being that is never content with the status quo but rather always looking for a better way, which leads to continual learning. The disposition to always engage in learning creates the entry point for the rigorous efforts to understand and take on new ways of practice.

An exciting realization occurred for many of us who work in coaching and staff development when we began to identify specific frameworks used to teach children that are transferable to the structure of work with adults. For instance, strategies originally adapted for reading comprehension were proving valuable for understanding new ways of approaching teaching. While conveying the steps for the gradual release of responsibility model for working with students, we were actually using that same sequence with the teachers. Through modeling, practice, and reflection, adults, like children, took in new information, mulled it over, and made it their own.

The yearning for growth must be answered with an effective process and valid content for learning. With this explicit model in mind, I have cognitive understandings, tools, and strategies to support the implementation of my beliefs about teaching and learning. I can offer a framework to the leadership team who asked me to recommend a plan to improve the quality of teaching in their school. I have support for my unwavering belief that we can help all teachers find their greatness.

Chapter 2

First Considerations and Steps: Planning for Professional Learning

Implementation of instructional change is so deep and so varied that any initial agreements and understandings of how people see themselves in this process will make or break the initiative.

—Sam Bennett

Guiding Questions

What promised results would engage your interest in a particular model?
What change would you commit to as a learner?
What responsibility would you commit to hold in this process?
What is your preferred context for learning?

The first considerations and steps people make determine the quality and nature of the change process. It is most critical that the community members and the culture they have established hold and sustain a view of the desired destination. Belief in the ability and commitment of these school community members to manage their own change and learning provides the basis for authentic sustainable change.

What are the principles for this change when based not merely on training but rather in on-the-job teacher learning, with goals to understand, remember, and apply in the world? In *The Long Haul: An Autobiography* (1998), Myles Horton's experience learning from practiced hoboes how to ride the rails during the Great Depression became a sustaining metaphor for initiating social change.

> You visualize the pace in your mind, then you synchronize that with your steps so that you hit the ground with exactly the same speed. During practice, I fell two or three times because I didn't get it right. Whenever I fell, they just kept on saying, "You've got to feel it." You flow on the train; you flow off the train, just like water. If you get on a train that's going faster than you are, it will swing your body around, your legs will flop out. It'll knock your handgrips loose and you'll fall under the train. They didn't have any trouble convincing me that I'd better learn this, because I'd seen people thrown under the tracks. . . . There's an artistry to it all that most people don't understand. The hoboes would warn people, "Don't just think that anybody can catch a freight train, you can get off the freight train and get killed." . . . These experiences helped me think about the pace of social change and how to treat it. (83)

At that time in his story, many people were searching for work wherever they could find it. They had to keep moving, following rumors of work in other places. They took those leaps onto speeding trains in order to get to the next town, the next state, wherever they could find an adequate livelihood and make their lives okay again.

In education, we are also taking leaps—in our search for the right strategies, the right program, and the right approach— so that all the children will learn and everyone's life will be okay. We run to catch up to the latest trend, the latest program or structure, the newest training. And too often we, or the program, miss the perfect flow and fall under the tracks, and the innovation is left behind. Then we get up and look for the next new idea to get us where we want to go.

Whenever a new professional development effort begins, whether it arises from the school community or from a decision made at a higher level in the system, teachers are best served when they are clear about their purpose, needs, and goals and when the ownership and responsibility for reaching the destination remain explicitly and authentically in their hands. The teachers are ultimately the ones who will do the leaping. They have to believe in the work and it has to fit within their set of beliefs and practices.

Acknowledging strength and value already in place— recognizing that there already is, to one extent or another, a place of knowledge and learning as the point of departure— is crucial. New learning that integrates and builds on what is already working leads to progress.

Determining Sources for Learning

> You cannot teach a person anything. You can only help him find it for himself.
>
> —Galileo

Like the hoboes in Myles Horton's story leaping on and off speeding trains, we need to proceed mindfully, under the guidance of those more experienced, as we leap toward instructional change, lest our handgrips get knocked loose and we are thrown under the tracks.

Whether made by or for teachers a decision to embark on a road to school improvement inevitably leads to the next steps:

- determining what learning is needed to reach the destination
- determining what resources are fitting and available

Knowing the school community's needs, teachers' goals, interests, and preferred learning styles helps in determining which resources are appropriate for their situation. Generally, there are resources right inside their own buildings and district as well as from outside organizations, programs, and consultants.

Colleagues

> Iron sharpens iron.
>
> —Old folk saying

For many years, there has been a growing trend to support the value of collaborative or collegial learning arrangements. Within every school, there is a tremendous, often untapped resource in each teacher's strengths, talents, experience, and trainings that could be shared.

Presenting what has been successful, observing each other's teaching, and planning together are powerful means for teacher learning. Teachers may be hesitant to step forward in this way lest they be seen as declaring themselves better than the group, but when such strategies are presented as collegial learning, the expectation is clear that everyone has something to share and something to learn. When teachers learn from each other, there is a gain not only in individual teacher effectiveness, but also in consistency across classrooms and coherence in the school culture (see Figure 2–1).

There are many formats that allow colleagues to safely and effectively share what they know and do well.

- Study groups and grade- and cross-grade-level team meetings provide opportunities to share ideas and experiences that promote collegial respect and shared knowledge.
- Faculty meetings can be structured so that teachers have a forum to share successes and initiate conversations around similar themes and ideas.
- Observations made in each other's classrooms build trust and engender common knowledge of all students' experiences at school.

Each of these interactions promotes a culture where it is understood that everyone learns from everyone. With growing comfort, teachers begin to spontaneously seek out opportunities to share their excitement or questions with colleagues as they arise.

At Base Line Middle School, Larry Runnels, the eighth-grade history teacher, and Mary Jo Bode, the language arts teacher, team teach a combined class for a popular course they

---

Survey for Collegial Learning

Name _____

Please respond to the following questions so we can develop a plan for collegial learning.

What training in instruction or content have you attended that led you to new or more effective classroom practice?

What teaching or learning ideas are you excited about?

What do you have considerable experience with that you have held onto and done each year because it works with kids?

What are you reading that is provoking questions, new thinking, or new practice?

What would you be interested in exploring with your colleagues?

Figure 2–1: *A survey distributed among teachers to gather information about what they can offer to colleagues or what they would like to explore is often the first step toward a plan for collaborative learning.*

call "Histlish." When the seventh-grade team met with staff developers for long-range planning, Mary Jo joined the group to share what she and Larry had learned and developed in their class over the years. She shared her methods for teaching research skills in history, literacy strategies for understanding texts, and communication skills for students to demonstrate their learning. From this meeting, the seventh-grade teachers gained both valuable ideas for their teaching and more understanding of eighth-grade expectations. For Mary Jo, this was an opportunity to articulate and reflect on the details as well as the big picture of what she and Larry provide for the students in their classroom. As a result of this collaborative discussion, seventh-grade social studies and language arts teachers, Zeke Tiernan and Jackie Hockney decided to further integrate and coordinate literacy skills to support the process of learning geography content. Their principal, Candy Hyatt, found a small planning grant so they could develop a plan for their two classes. Because they had heard from a respected colleague about the purpose and benefits of team teaching as well as specific steps for implementing a plan, and because their principal provided logistical and moral support, they were able to commit to an action plan to implement new learning and ideas.

When teachers learn from each other's innovations, professional development, that is, ongoing learning, becomes embedded in the faculty's everyday teaching life. In this way, a successful program can genuinely take root and spread into another area of the school building.

District Coaches

I often see myself as a bridge.

—Caroline McKinney, district coach for Boulder Valley Schools

Many districts have been expanding the in-house instructional support they provide for teachers through a range of context-specific coaching opportunities to address particular district goals for students. Expertise in teaching second language learners, mentoring for new teachers, and coaching in math, science, and literacy instruction are just a few of the areas in which districts provide assistance. With their wealth of experience and understanding, these coaches, who are usually former teachers, provide ideas and modeling for current best instructional practice. They also bring the weight and influence of the district—communicating district, and even state, agendas that affect practice in the classroom and interpreting directives with recommendations that support the individual school.

Schools that most benefit from the presence of district coaches are those whose faculty members communicate honestly and regularly with the coach about what is and isn't working with their students. They also include the coach in the community so that she truly understands the context in order to offer appropriately helpful input. Principals provide logistical support through creating schedules that allow time for the coach to meet with faculty and participate in their after-school meetings. The coaches, in turn, bring a grounded knowledge of district expectations and support along with an attitude of exploration and respect for collaboration.

Caroline McKinney, a literacy coach for Boulder Valley School District in Boulder, Colorado, writes a monthly letter, "Caroline's Corner," for the teachers in the three buildings in which she works. Just before the beginning of state testing one year, she wrote the following to the teachers at Heatherwood Elementary School:

Happy Almost March!

I know many of you are deeply involved in the CSAP [Colorado State Assessment Program]. That means additional time spent on test prep (reading directions, looking for key words, envisioning the writing, brainstorming ideas and drafts). One of the lessons I have learned from being with your students is that they seem to enjoy writing to prompts as long as they still have choice and voice! So, although I'm working with many of you on these kinds of test-taking mini-lessons, I keep returning to my writing heroes for wisdom and perspective. Ralph Fletcher, Katie Wood Ray, and Shelley Harwayne continue to inspire me with their insights about the real writing children can do . . . and how we can teach craft.

She continues to expand to other ideas related specifically to the range of concerns and questions she has heard in her regular work with teachers and children in the building. In her role and with her expertise, Caroline is in a position to offer teachers a view of instruction that is both practical and inspirational. She offers a pathway to incorporate the multiplicity of responsibilities she experiences and shares right alongside the teachers.

In order to identify support that is available and valuable for your school from the district, it can be helpful to gather responses from the faculty (see Figure 2–2).

Professional Development Organizations and Consultants

I truly love your ideas . . . it is certainly a fresh perspective that forces me to extend beyond how I teach.

—Excerpt from email written by social studies teacher Sangita Patel
to staff developer Sam Bennett

Like Caroline McKinney, the best staff developers I have seen offer specific skills, strategies, and tools, and also bring new energy and attitudes that encourage teachers to explore, take risks and sustain hope. Knowing that someone from the outside is checking in and holding the vision, even when ultimate ownership and commitment are maintained within the school building, helps sustain focused momentum.

Sometimes, teachers view the entrance of a professional development or school reform program as an indication that their teaching is inadequate. In other professions, such as medicine, it is accepted that new knowledge, understandings, and techniques are continually being discovered and developed, and keeping current with the cutting edge ideas is vital to the profession. One of the primary roles of an outside consultant might be to further the professionalism of teachers by

Questions to Gather Information
About District Resources

Name _____

In order to identify support that is available and valuable for your school from the district, we would like to gather your responses to the following questions:

What are the particular needs at your school right now?

Who do you think of at the district with expertise in these areas?

What do you see as the particular strengths of individuals from the district office assigned to your school?

Who do you think would be best to communicate with the district and coaches and coordinate interaction?

Figure 2–2: *In order to identify support that is available and valuable for your school from the district, it's helpful to gather responses from the faculty to these questions.*

bringing the newest ideas and research to supplement and inform what teachers already know and do well.

There has been an unexamined assumption that if the staff developers "do their job," they will not be needed forever. This could be a misconception. If professional development is merely training, then teachers do learn discrete steps and activities and continue on their own. But if the staff developer's role is to bring outside views and cutting-edge research and thinking, and to watch for the next steps toward excellence, then she is an unending source of assistance.

Creating a Working Relationship

When school communities choose professional learning, they are faced with a staggering number of programs and initiatives offering widely varying options. The number of school reform organizations and individual consultants seems to increase every day. The roles of staff developers can range from trainer and presenter to consultant, planner, and facilitator. They are called on to facilitate meetings or professional development days, to assist various groups in problem solving, or to consult with development of long-range plans. The scope of their programs and processes is vast—from scripted lesson plans with specific time frames to follow throughout the day, to the individually crafted, process-oriented development of each teacher's capacity.

The approach that staff developers, coaches, trainers, or program representatives recommend for teaching children usually mirrors the approach they use to teach the model to adults. Similarly, the beliefs that faculty members hold about learning determine the choices they make for their students and for themselves. If given a choice, they tend to choose programs or approaches that fit into their stated or unstated cultural norms.

Determining the resources that best fit faculty members' particular goals in terms of content and process is the beginning and the foundation of the school's change process.

Clearly deciding which resources and learning processes they prefer as learners requires layers of information gathered from essential questions.

These questions lead to appropriate structures, time frames, and activities that will need to be planned for when the effort begins (see Figure 2–3).

Initial conversations usually revolve around the possibilities for a working partnership between the school and the professional development organization; specifically, determining how the organization's work will serve the school's purpose.

The teachers at Witt Elementary in Westminster, Colorado, were directed by their district to choose a literacy-based staff development program. They believed in their own capacity to discover and implement new learning as much as they believed in the students' ability to learn and grow. They took an active role in determining the partnerships and direction of their staff development.

Coaches and consultants may enter with their own view of what needs to happen. All stakeholders should be honest and as clear as possible about their beliefs and agenda from the beginning. I once worked in a school that adhered to a philosophy nearly diametrically opposed to my own. After a year of struggle, we finally had to acknowledge that though we shared a common devotion to our profession and to children, our beliefs about approach were too divergent to find a common meeting point. Since they were interested in the instructional model, we decided it would be more useful for them to go to lab classrooms, see the work in real settings and then figure out among themselves how to translate it to their school culture. Looking back, I wonder if, had we allowed more time and opportunity in the beginning for all stakeholders to consider options, we might have avoided a possibly wasted year.

Resistance and confusion often arise when the application interview and decision-making process is not thorough or inclusive of a representative group of school community members. I've found myself in buildings where the teachers had no

---

Questions to Assess Professional Development Resources

What does this model identify as school needs and potential results?

What will be expected of the school in order to achieve the results?

What does the organization promise to do toward meeting specific school goals?

What results does the organization promise and in what time frame?

What structures and understandings will support sustaining the change after the contracted time ends?

Figure 2–3: *Questions to Assess Professional Development Resources*

idea who I was or what I might do for them. They weren't necessarily interested in another outside "program" to fit in with the many they were already learning. In those schools, the first year is often spent searching for a point of need, a spark of interest, and a place to fit into their goals.

To obtain an accurate and sufficient picture, it is most helpful for school community members to observe the work of the organization in practice:

- Pay a visit to a school already working with the organization under consideration.
- Talk with teachers and principals who have worked with the organization.
- Contract for a few days of staff development with an identified focus.

Bringing someone in to provoke and support change carries risk as well as potential benefits. It reminds me of a program I heard about for troubled families where a social worker comes in to live with them, watch their dynamics, and then offer recommendations to improve the parenting. As a parent, I would want to be sure that the person's knowledge base and point of view fit with mine. It is essential to acknowledge the inherent choice and responsibility that resides with the learner when true actionable learning is the goal.

Chapter 3

Community Dynamics:
Individuals and Their Relationships

*Myles Horton's grandfather said, "You can hitch your wagon to
the stars, but you can't haul corn or hay in it if its wheels
aren't on the ground."*

—Myles Horton, *The Long Haul: An Autobiography*

Guiding Questions

Who has influence, power, or control over instructional
practice in the school?
What do you have control over in your own instructional
practice?
What are the dynamics in collegial relationships that everyone
knows but no one discusses publicly?
How do the dynamics impact the ability of individuals and the
school community to improve instruction for students?
What agreements could be established to move through these
dynamics?
What are the logistics for instructional support and
leadership?

While initial conversations about school improvement ostensibly identify purpose and need, they often lean
toward great hopes and dreams "hitched to the stars" for the
work ahead. Real chances for success lie in getting the "wheels
on the ground," that is, in figuring out the details particular to
each situation and considering the time, energy, and capacity
necessary for taking steps on unfamiliar paths.

A Continuum of Participation

The nature of the first steps and pace with which the school will move ahead in its change efforts is a delicate issue and depends on the dynamics and relationships of the people involved. Teachers asked to implement changes are like actors who are suddenly told in the middle of a performance that they must use a revised or perhaps even completely new script with many spaces for ad-libbing and improvisation, and that they must make the shift while the audience is watching. People have varying degrees of comfort with that kind of on-the-job change. While there are some people who prefer the thrill of improvisation and interactive theatre, many others need time to learn the script and understand the whole play before they can bring it to life on the stage.

For those people who want more time to think and observe, perhaps to understand, the essence of the new "script" before they try it in their classrooms, chances for success and positive experiences diminish if they are pushed to take action before they are ready. While they might appear to comply, they will not have the necessary investment to actually change their instructional practice.

Unfortunately, these people are often viewed negatively as resisters. In reality, as long as they are considering and observing and not ignoring or sabotaging, their position is not negative at all. People who question and challenge often express valid concern or the opinions of others who don't want to speak publicly. They might be people who think very carefully and when they join, it will be with a steadfast commitment. If they are acknowledged and validated for their views, resisters often reveal where the new growth will occur. As Michael Fullan wrote in *Change Forces: The Sequel* (1999), "Reform often misfires because we fail to learn from those who disagree with us."

Points of entry for each individual will be different, so it is essential that multiple options be made available. Through discussion and/or through observation, the values and beliefs held by individuals and collectively in the school can be explicitly identified.

Specific questions to identify entry points or gateways are varied. Fully exploring questions from the following list can provide a base from which individuals and school faculty can identify where and how they will begin. A whole faculty could consider the complete list by dividing into small groups, with each group taking one question and then reporting their essential ideas back to the whole group. Guiding questions for this early exploration can include:

- What are the predominant as well as dissenting views expressed?
- What are the beliefs about the students' capacity to learn?
- On what evidence, experience, tradition, or intuition are the beliefs based?
- What is the capacity for taking risks and trying something new?
- What assessments are used to evaluate student learning? Which assessments do the teachers use to inform their teaching decisions?
- What is the stance on covering mandated curriculum?
- What pressures and goals are held in regard to standardized test scores?
- What are the significant pressures and goals to increase student achievement?
- What beliefs do those in positions of leadership hold about teachers' capacity to learn and teach effectively?

There are many factors involved in creating the appropriate balance of risk taking and safety. Leaders of the effort such as staff developers, administrators, and teachers need to be careful that they neither push so hard that people get run over nor go so easy that momentum is never achieved.

A continuum of participation allows each individual to identify the first step where he is comfortable in the beginning of the effort. This could range from the most minimal involvement such as participating in discussions at faculty meetings to trying new strategies in the classroom (see Figure 3–1).

Continuum of Participation

Your name _____

I would like to participate in professional learning in the following way(s):

Read and discuss

- Articles
- Book(s)

During

- Already scheduled faculty meeting time
- After school meeting

Observe

- Demonstration lessons at school
- Classrooms at other schools
- Attend lab (4 visits to the same classroom over the year)

Implement new instructional strategies in my classroom

- Staff developer demonstration lessons in my classroom
- Plan and co-teach with staff developer

Ongoing Collaborative Learning

- Peer observations
- Critical Friends Group looking at student work and instructional practice

What instructional practice or strategies are you particularly interested in learning more about?

- Reading comprehension
- Gradual Release of Responsibility (modeling/think-aloud, scaffolding for guided and independent practice)
- Workshop structure for classroom
- Specific subject area: reading, writing, math, science
- Experiential concept-based curriculum planning and instruction
- Other

Additional ideas, questions, requests

Figure 3–1: *Continuum of Participation*

There is a dilemma faced among coaches and staff developers about "getting to everybody" no matter their level of commitment versus working deeply with a few, who can then serve as models for their colleagues. The key is that everyone is included—continually aware of the new ideas, continually invited to participate (through conversations as well as distributed menus), and consistently hearing from colleagues about classroom experiences (see Figure 3–2).

Contours of Leadership

> Instead of looking for saviors we should be calling for leadership that will challenge us to face problems of which there are no simple painless solutions—problems that require us to learn in new ways. (Heifitz 1994)

When the responsibility and desire for professional development reside in the school community rather than, or at least alongside, an outside consultant, structures and individuals are essential to maintain that responsibility. First, a plan for ongoing engaged participation is vital, regardless of the physical presence of coaches or staff developers.

Teacher-Leaders

Finding teachers eager to take the first leap is often the key to getting started. The influence of such a core group, who can then show evidence of results for students, is one way to ensure sustainable momentum. This impact is reinforced when students carry certain skills and expectations for learning from one grade to another, or in secondary schools to another class.

These core teachers usually identify themselves through their expressed interest in professional development opportunities and willingness to try new practices in the classroom. A customized plan for each teacher is based on:

- their own descriptive assessment of practice
- samples of student work
- formal observations from colleagues, administrators, or coaches

---

Ways to Participate in Professional Development: A Menu

Learning from Colleagues

- Observe in each other's classrooms
- Plan and debrief with colleagues
- Look at student work together using protocols
- Eat lunch together to talk about what you've done in your class and what you're thinking
- Try things in your classroom and talk with colleagues

Study Groups

- Professional literature: articles or books
- Personal reading: articles or books; fiction or nonfiction
- Burning issue or common theme
- Regular team meetings around topic or reading

Practicing in Your Classroom

- Explicitly focus on strategy throughout classroom
- Teach strategy during reading instruction: Use instructional model; gradual release of responsibility
- Notice your own reading strategies and share with students
- Try strategies in other subject areas

Figure 3–2: *Ways to Participate in Professional Development: A Menu*

Working with Staff Developers or Coaches

- Observe demonstration lessons in your own or other classrooms
- Consult on planning
- Co-teach

Networking

- Visit other schools or classrooms
- Attend labs
- Attend classes or seminars

Going Public

- Share what you've done that worked or about which you have questions
- Provide demonstrations for colleagues
- Display student work in public spaces
- Present student work for focused discussion

Assessment

- Journal of your own thinking and learning
- Running records
- Regular conferencing with students
- Asset map
- Portfolios: student, teacher, school
- Anecdotal observations of children's progress

Figure 3–2: *Ways to Participate in Professional Development: A Menu* (continued)

At Prairie Middle School, after the initial introductions, my colleague Sam Bennett and I had had three meetings with the team most interested in working with us. In these meetings, we studied student work samples and talked about effective instruction. When we finally visited the classrooms, our eyes were opened to the realities of these teachers' strengths and challenges. When we observed Jeff Cazier's science class, Sam and I were struck by his intuitive though inconsistent use of cognitive strategies and best practice instruction. We recorded every strategy he used that fit into our list of best practice instruction (including specific use of strategies to support thinking). And we noted when he didn't follow these structures (such as a work assignment that created confusion for the students).

When we met with Jeff after school, we described the effective strategies he had instinctively been using as well as omissions in his lesson that confused the students. We could nearly see the light go on in his head. "You mean, I was doing all those things without realizing it? You could help me to consciously do those things more consistently?" Jeff's enthusiasm sparked the whole team, who began popping with possibilities for how this cognitive awareness of best practices could help them pointedly and intentionally increase their efficacy with students. Subsequent observations in each teacher's classroom led to a plan based on a mutual assessment of specific needs and goals—where they were (current state) and where they needed and wanted to go (desired state). Their interest and commitment drove and sustained the initiative at their school. As they began to identify visible results for students, other teachers in the school became interested in learning more about what they were doing. The following year, with support and encouragement from school administrators, the teachers from this team moved into formally recognized leadership roles in the school's professional development design.

Formal Roles for Teacher Leaders

While individuals often emerge who carry the torch for an initiative, without formal support they may not be able to sustain the time and energy necessary to carry that responsibility.

Some schools—and some professional development programs—designate an individual, who is freed from other duties, to act as liaison or coordinator. In-school coordinators or liaisons are usually responsible for:

- continuing the effort in between staff developer visits;
- connecting individual programs to the whole school;
- coordinating logistics and schedules; and
- providing information and a context for staff developers' experience on their intermittent visits.

A person in this capacity can lead a team that acts as a bridge between school faculty and outside consultants. By breaking down the perception of an extra, outside program added to what occurs in the school every day, the perception becomes that of an ongoing effort led by faculty members.

Principals

Achievement of any goal is more likely when philosophical and logistical support comes from the lead administrator. Since everyone relies on the principal to carry the big-picture view, it is helpful and possibly essential that she articulate and believe in the professional learning model as a fundamental aspect of the school's overall achievement.

Current job expectations for principals require that they be instructional leaders who understand instruction and learning, stay current on best practice research and literature, and be inspired facilitators and adamant advocates for their community. The principal must manage in a way that provides logistical support for learning and change by arranging for release time for discussion, faculty meetings, and inservice days focused on instruction; and by filtering external pressures so teachers can concentrate on best instructional practice. Principals also manage budgets and seek funding for particular projects that make teachers' growth and enriched activities in the classrooms a possibility. The creativity of a determined principal is an awesome force.

Without the principal's support and commitment, the initiative may continue in isolated pockets for a period of time but eventually the spark to continue will fade. Many times the principal who makes an initial commitment is not there to see it through. At one middle school with a large at-risk population, a new principal arrived after the contract and grant for professional development had been signed. She had her own beliefs about what goals were most important and how to achieve the goals for students. Teachers became confused by the conflicting messages and dropped out of our program. For a while, a few key individuals continued to show an interest in meeting to talk about instruction but the application to classroom practice was limited, and professional development work became more marginalized. We were able to continue to work with these teachers but with a more limited expectation for the scope of impact.

In contrast, Ellin Keene recalls that at Foster Elementary, where everyone moved forward together, principal Joy Hood "really had the steering wheel. . . . She said, 'I want you to do this.' . . . Her level of involvement was central to our team because we were all focused on the same thing." Underlying Joy's support was a determined belief in the identified goals for student learning.

Similarly, at Aspen Creek, principal Scott Winston's commitment is also based on his deep beliefs about teaching and learning. Increased mandates and pressures from the district, as well as unexpected crises accompanying opening a new building forced him to revise his time line but left his ultimate commitment and support unshaken.

I have observed that the principals whose schools have shown the most progress in any endeavor are those who fight for everything the students need and who model the belief that their schools will succeed. They usually work on multiple fronts, building strong relationships with those who wield power and influence over the schools' resources and balancing support for and pressure on teachers' performance. This stance can often put them in precarious positions. Staff developers and teacher leaders can provide crucial coaching that sustains a principal's efforts to obtain essential school needs.

Customs and Habits

Every school community I have watched successfully implement new practice has been willing to acknowledge and grapple with cultural habits and relationships. If they don't, ingrained dynamics of mistrust and opposition will deflect forward movement and ultimately sabotage any efforts to progress. Similarly, staff developers must become deeply involved with people in the school to uncover personal habits and relationships that prevent the free and open discussion of essential ideas. Often, they touch on sore points; tension, discord, or conflict is almost inevitable.

As a staff developer new to a school, I sometimes feel as if I am walking through a field of land mines, trying to sense where the explosives might be buried so I can safely defuse them. I know I can't just avoid them or, worse, pretend they're not there. In the school culture of one elementary school, people did not pull punches with each other or with staff developers. Although many of the teachers were enthusiastic, a small group expressed dissatisfaction and frustration in the early stages of professional development. One teacher slipped us a note asking for opportunities to leave anonymous feedback. Another walked out on a lesson instead of staying to debrief. They tried to rally support to express their anger as a whole faculty. They had conversations with their principal.

These were dedicated, sincere teachers who were experiencing heartfelt discomfort and concern. They felt that the process was not working for their learning and they wanted to learn. For the teachers who were finding value, for the staff developers and administrators, it was tempting to dismiss their concern as a result of their own personal issues rather than a consequence of our efforts. A balance point had to be found, where disgruntled teachers were heard and attended to but did not take over. The whole community was painfully affected by this dynamic, and each member of the school team responded.

- The principal listened to everyone's voices. He met with teachers individually and listened to their concerns. He restated that the school's commitment to progress would be sustained regardless of the current turmoil.
- Teachers publicly voiced the valuable learning and changes that had occurred in their practice and that were already resulting in increased learning and engagement for students.
- Staff developers persevered in their work with teachers and students, did not take the anger or criticisms personally, continued to listen and respond to all voices, and took extra time to talk with and build stronger relationships with all individuals.

As a whole school team, we wanted to prevent one group from splintering into an isolated disenfranchised faction, so we worked hard to stay connected with each other. We spent more time establishing personal trust and respect for each other's knowledge and considered everyone's current concerns, to show that the well-being of individuals did matter. By fearlessly facing this turmoil, which had already been present among the faculty and by continuing the work in classrooms, we built mutual trust. As staff developers, we survived a complex initiation into the community.

By the end of the year, at the last inservice, everyone joined in with a spirit of open hearts and collaboration, newly amenable and receptive. Specific steps were identified in team meetings and plans were laid for the following year.

Next Steps for Upcoming School Year

- Preschool summer institute: Starting out as a community: content and process for planning and building strong working relationships
- Business handled by staff council and email communications so meetings can be focused on instruction
- Monthly faculty meeting dedicated to study group
- Monthly team-planning time facilitated with study/discussion focused on instruction: books, themes, looking at student work
- Student work displays in designated spot—rotate grade levels; student work on website
- Continuum of involvement: study groups/discussions, labs, school visits, co-teach with staff developers; observations of your teaching
- Develop a version of the asset map based on site-specific goals. Monthly anecdotal evidence recorded at faculty meetings
- Assessment: pre– and post–data collection

Valuable insights into the realities of the school community— the land mines were at least charted—prevented further clumsy steps onto unexploded mines.

Sometimes it takes a while for the tension to become evident. After an encouraging meeting with a whole faculty before they opened a brand-new building, the first day of school was delayed by two weeks because construction wasn't complete. When school did open, clocks didn't work, bells didn't ring, the heat was unpredictable, supplies weren't all delivered, and basic procedures for running the school were not established. With their focus on providing stable first days for the students, the faculty reeled from the realities of a school that didn't have established community routines and rules. During this period of basic survival and development, there was little energy available to endure the discomfort of looking at and pushing instructional practices. Many people wanted to hold on to what they had done in their previous schools, which included maintaining existing collegial relationships. They said they needed to find solid ground before they could handle the disequilibrium of changing their customary instructional practices.

Limited introductions and demonstration classes were provided so that everyone could see a common picture of an instructional model. With the idea of slowly building momentum with volunteers, Anne Goudvis and I offered support with discrete lessons or units for teachers who expressed an interest.

At the end of that school year, discord emerged at a faculty meeting. Some teachers thought there was an "in group" of involved teachers. While Anne and I were taken aback by this reaction, we had seen it before. Even when teachers voluntarily stay on the sidelines, they worry or perceive that they have missed something.

The teachers' discomfort could have led to a crisis. Instead, it was cause for celebration—for three reasons:

1. The teachers felt safe enough to express their dissatisfaction to the whole group rather than in whispered hallway conversations, which could lead to further fracturing and undermining.
2. The administration was alerted to an underlying issue that potentially could undermine the establishment of the new school community.
3. Teachers saw, in their own time frame, a potential value in the instructional model.

By the second year, more teachers had had positive experiences to report, and the perception of embedded ongoing professional learning with a place for everyone began to develop.

By the third year, when I walked through the building on my first day back, I was welcomed with hugs. By returning year after year and, most of all, by listening to teachers and working *with* rather than *on* them, our presence became an expected part of their community and professional lives in the following ways:

- Teachers knew what to expect in terms of working relationships and direction.
- Everyone had at least engaged in conversations and listened to colleagues present new ideas that led to new results for students.
- Many teachers added new strategies and processes to their repertoire for teaching.
- Teachers had a chance to build on learning step-by-step over the years and see developing results for children.

Commitment to the professional relationship between a staff developer and an individual teacher can take the work to deep levels of collaboration. Sam Bennett recounts her experience of initiation with one teacher in her journal. She describes the teacher, Sangita Patel as, "an extremely hard-working social studies teacher . . . with an amazing passion for history . . . and an incredible dedication to bringing it alive for students. . . . She works weekends and holidays, attends every meeting and usually attends any learning opportunity that crosses her path." Sam describes the rich theatrical environment Sangita creates in her room along with her serious commitment to follow district mandates for standards and curriculum.

Sam writes, "Because of Sangita's belief in the content standards and her dedication to doing her job well, Marjorie and I knew immediately that our biggest challenge with Sangita would be helping her to slow down with the content and teach for understanding instead of always trying to meet the goal of 'coverage.'"

Sam describes "hitting a rough patch" a few months into the first year of staff development. While observing in Sangita's classroom, Sam realized the students were lost. She decided to help them make a personal connection to enhance their understanding and grasp of the content. She writes, "I blurted out, 'Has anyone ever driven from here to Las Vegas?' Sangita looked up in shock. It was very hard for her to have me speak aloud and she perceived that I was 'taking over' her classroom. I persisted for a few minutes and the kids got pretty lively. . . . After school we had a chance to debrief and Sangita talked about how uncomfortable it made her feel to have me interrupt the flow of her lesson. Fortunately she said that she had noticed the increased engagement of the students and had tried it with her afternoon students and it had worked . . . I saw an opportunity to push her thinking even further by challenging her about her packets and use of worksheets. I just kept asking, 'Why?' and 'Are they getting it? How do you know?' She was so frustrated that she shut down."

The next time Sam and Sangita saw each other was on a visit to Carole Quinby's fifth-grade classroom at Harrington Elementary School where Sangita and her team would have a chance to see what had previously only been described. Sangita greeted Sam "with a forgiving smile and a hug and said she needed help . . . I jumped at the chance and we set a date for later the following week." The project they planned that day became an anchor point for Sangita to refer back to in order to remember what worked so well with her students. She and Sam both also refer back to their "rough patch" with a comradely chuckle, acknowledging how they stuck with each other through a hard time that ended up taking them further into their work than they might have imagined possible. This was not the last time that Sangita, or her teammates, were pushed beyond their level of comfort, but it was the last time they perceived the push as a breakdown rather than another step forward in the process.

Each of these stories illustrates the same sequence for the initial breakthrough:

- Genuine interest in an articulated idea for improving instruction
- Congenial relationships at the beginning
- Open expression of discomfort or resistance

- Perseverance through a struggle
- New understandings and change in practice
- Continued relationships that go deeper into the work and learning

Underlying the ability and capacity to "stick with it" through the cognitive dissonance of those hard times is a combination of a body of knowledge based on research and experience, a clear picture for teacher learning, a belief in the possibility of success, and a few anchor individuals to see results and provide evidence of the value of their experience and the joy in the work.

Chapter 4

A Framework for Professional Learning

If you tell them, they'll watch your lips move. If you show them, they'll want to do it themselves.

—Maria Montessori

Guiding Questions

What opportunities can I find to see as well as hear about new effective instructional strategies?

What opportunities can we arrange that provide time to think and reflect about new effective instructional strategies and practice in classrooms as well as the whole school?

How can I explore and try out new ideas in real-life teaching situations?

What do I teach that I love to do?

What do I ask my students to do that I would resist doing myself?

Why would I resist it?

What do I wish I could do better?

What support, such as opportunities to see models and/or opportunities for discussion, would help me stretch beyond this limitation?

Principles of best practice instruction for children (as defined by the teachers embarked on new learning) will be embedded, whether implicitly or explicitly, in an effective instructional framework for adults. For instance, using gradual release of responsibility as a model for instruction and cognitive strategies that support thinking and learning, everyone understands the road they will follow. Teachers have multiple opportunities to see instructional demonstrations, practice with guidance, and reflect and respond. Optional side trips and rest stops will appear along the way, but the main path remains visible. Teachers know from the beginning that independent practice, or application, is their desired destination.

As a staff developer and as a teacher, I regularly ask myself three guiding questions to determine what I am going to do:

1. How can I show, as well as describe, what I am trying to convey?
2. How can I provide opportunities for everyone to think and reflect about what it means for the individual teacher/learner?
3. How can I support application of learning to real-life situations?

Modeling

> What I learned from my mentor: . . . model, model, model.
>
> —Carrie Symons' reflection on learning to be an effective teacher

After providing background content and context; articulating purpose, need, and expectations; and getting to know a little about each other, I provide multiple ways for teachers to see and experience what has been promised: actual pictures and models of what "it" looks like when the teaching and learning goals are achieved.

Demonstration Lessons and Co-teaching

Description: A tightly focused, purposefully planned session that provides an opportunity for teachers to see a particular instructional strategy, usually in the context of their own classroom or school.

Purpose: Demonstration lessons observed by a group of teachers provide common ground for a facilitated discussion on specific instructional strategies and their impact on student learning. Demonstration lessons also play a key introductory role. They quickly establish credibility and trust between

47

coaches and teachers by showing teachers that the coach is willing to put herself on the line and work with their students in the actual setting.

Most powerfully, demonstrations show what is possible with the same students the teacher works with in his classroom. Ellin Keene, a master of demonstration lessons, advises, "The emphasis that is crucial in the demonstration lessons is the rigor, pushing the students' thinking, by constantly saying, in effect, 'What else? What else? What else?'" With that emphasis in her mind, Ellin's demonstration of children's capacity to think and learn expands everyone's view of what students might achieve.

Structures and Logistics: Demonstration lessons can range from pure theatre in which one or more teachers watch someone else teach, to a model of total teacher participation. In any case, teachers must be actively engaged as participant observers.

The most effective structure for a demonstration lesson includes the teachers in the planning so they learn about the thinking underlying the instructional activity and behavior. They can also then contribute to building the lesson to fit their students' knowledge and needs. Planning for demonstration lessons includes a carefully articulated focus for both adult and student learning as well as specific replicable instructional behaviors and strategies that will be shown (see Figure 4–1).

During the demonstration, the purpose is teacher learning through focused observation and discussion. To this end, the demonstrator may pause during a lesson, ask the students to excuse the interruption, and address the observing teachers to help them:

- See the behavior and strategies. *Example: "What I am doing right now is showing . . ."*
- Name what might be noticed in the students' responses. *Example: "Do you see how they . . . ?"*
- Raise questions to consider for subsequent discussions. *Example: "What do you think . . . ?"*

Planning Demonstration Lessons

Instructional Focus:
- For Teacher
- For Student(s)

Instructional Strategy to Be Demonstrated:

Scaffold/Structures/Activities:

Questions to Explore:

Figure 4–1: *Planning Demonstration Lessons*

- Suggest a new focal point for the observation. *Example: "I'm noticing . . . and I'd be interested in exploring . . . "*

These focusing prompts also provide reference points for note taking and for the debrief conversation after the observation.

Demonstration lessons can vary in terms of teacher participation. Once I have established a working relationship with teachers, I begin co-teaching with them rather than demonstrating while they just watch. At first, I may lead the teaching and welcome teacher contributions to the discussion. Then the teacher and I may model a discussion of our thinking about a text. As the relationship grows, it becomes natural to play off each other in the teaching time, asking questions, challenging opinions, and providing feedback.

Eventually, I plan demonstration lessons as integral parts of ongoing projects or units, with teacher follow-through, rather than isolated demonstrations of discrete aspects of instruction. Along with demonstrations of specific strategies for teaching and learning, the building of knowledge and skills is made visible through demonstrations of lessons in context.

Facilitation: What are often called demonstration lessons are actually a sequence of learning events of which classroom teaching demonstration is one central part. The focused thinking, wondering, and connecting that occurs in discussion around that central part are the pieces that lead to implementation and understanding. Reflection and discussion around actual classroom work are the heart and soul of substantive staff development.

A facilitator for this discussion can help point out what occurred, what students were doing, and the significant details of the demonstrating teacher's strategies. This arrangement helps to formalize the experience with a purposeful focus. Recognizing limitations inherent in facilitating a debrief of one's own demonstration lesson, when there are two staff developers working together in a school, one may teach the lesson while the other facilitates the observation and debrief.

In a debrief session with teachers after the demonstration lesson, the discussion can help participating teachers to:

- Identify what learning occurred for the students. *Examples: "Every student was able to look at the page they read in the textbook as it connected to the whole chapter as well as at text structure clues for specific information." "All students refined their questions to give purpose to their reading." "They synthesized the information by putting it in their own words with double-column note taking."*

- Explore what worked well and what we might change next time. *Examples: "The students appeared confused when they were left to complete the organizer on their own." "Next time, look at the organizer again with students to make sure the steps and sequencing is clear." "Clearly state the expectation that the organizer is to help them hold the information for their own use." "Let students work in groups with teacher support when needed."*

- Commit to plans for follow-up and then prepare for the next demonstration. *Examples: "Teacher will continue using the prereading strategies with another kind of nonfiction text following the same steps." "The next demonstration lesson will help them choose and plan for text structures they will use to report their information."*

See Figure 4–2 for a simple structure to guide the thinking for the debrief of a demonstration.

In an effort to maximize learning, various formats and structures to sequence a demonstration lesson study are useful. A predetermined gradual release of responsibility to the teacher has three cycles:

1. Plan, demonstrate with teacher observing, debrief, plan
2. Co-teach, debrief, plan
3. Demonstrate with staff developer observing teacher, debrief, plan

---

Debrief of Demonstration Lesson

What learning occurred for the students?

What worked well and what would you do differently next time?

Plans for follow-up and next demonstration lesson.

Reflect on your own learning . . .

Figure 4–2: *Debrief of Demonstration Lesson*

Mariah Dickson, director of high school initiatives at PEBC, added further steps to the debrief and follow-up:

1. Plan with teachers
2. Teach the lesson with teachers observing
3. Debrief using a structured conversation to look at student work
4. Plan for follow-up based on what they saw in student work
5. Teacher follows up in classroom
6. Staff developer teaches another demonstration lesson

Demonstration lessons, especially in the beginning, are by nature limited in scope to clearly illustrate a particular focus requested by the classroom teacher. Repeated opportunities for demonstration lessons and debrief sessions provide the building blocks for an increasing body of skills and knowledge for effective instruction.

Independent Application: When demonstration lessons are successful and seen as valuable, teachers may want to continue in this first observing phase of the gradual release model where they see someone else teach. They often say how valuable it is to "just watch another person." Taking that next step to the guided practice phase is crucial to finding one's own particular way of fully integrating new practice into ongoing classroom practice. A clearly delineated plan supports genuine collaboration (see Figure 4–3).

At Aspen Creek, two sixth-grade teachers, Lisa Turner and Deanne Davies, agreed to set aside the weeks between Thanksgiving and winter break to work as a team in establishing authentic writer's workshop structures in their respective classrooms. We met three times to plan with the support of both the district literacy coach and the school literacy specialist. We wanted to create a model that incorporated all mandates, required assessments, and available resources.

With clear goals for student writing, we alternated the role of lead teacher. I modeled new strategies and key aspects for

---

Planning to Co-Teach

Goal:

Skills:

Content:

Genre/Text/Type of Inquiry:

Purpose:

Instructional Sequence:

Culminating Product:

Assessment:

Figure 4–3: *Planning to Co-Teach*

developing a community of writers in the classroom. Through one-on-one conferences with students, small group discussions on the writing process, and students' continual sharing of their writing, we tracked skill acquisition and application as well as motivation and engagement, and continually revised our plans.

Deanne and Lisa were able to concentrate on internalizing the essential systems, structures, and understandings so that when they moved on to the next unit of writing instruction, they continued using the same approach—now on their own.

Observations in Other Teachers' Classrooms
Journal Entry from Sarah Ballard, First Grade

February 27, 2003
Thursday

Today the visitors came agen. They are waching us writ. And read. They wach my techr listen to students. They walk around the room. And see how we are doing. They have notebooks. They writ in their notebooks.

Yearlong Labs

Description: Facilitated group observations of an exemplary teacher in her own classroom at another school on two or more occasions over a period of time from one week to a year.

Purpose: Labs offer teachers an opportunity to see what an instructional model provides for students over time. They can experience the atmosphere of the classroom and witness progress and struggles firsthand in authentic situations. Ample opportunity is provided to discuss what has been observed and the implications for participants' own school settings. Teachers can then identify specific aspects of the instructional model that they want to incorporate into their own work. Ideally, teachers attend with at least one colleague so that when they are back in their own schools, there is support to implement and share their learning.

Labs often present a particular instructional focus—a strategy such as for reading comprehension or a structure such as writer's workshop. The focus may also be in a content area or in a process for exploring content such as research on a topic of the Civil War. In secondary schools, where students spend their day with a whole team of teachers, the lab may take place in each individual classroom during a day or the teacher may demonstrate integration of subject and skill such as literacy in content areas.

Labs also provide possibilities for differentiated learning for participants. Each participant can observe and synthesize at his level of understanding. New teachers usually focus on one aspect such as classroom organization or the steps for a particular strategy. They must have the opportunity to ask all their questions and sift through everything to determine and develop the strategies and structures they will use. Experienced teachers can quickly identify ideas, strategies, and structures to add to their repertoire. Jan Nichols is a highly respected teacher at Douglas Elementary School in Boulder, Colorado, but after a lab in Lavonne Bird's classroom at Heatherwood Elementary School she completely rearranged her classroom furniture as well as core aspects of her teaching routines. In her final reflection, she wrote, "I have been invited to think about my teaching in a whole new way and with a different perspective. I want children to grow up to be wonderful thinkers and lovers of knowledge and learning. This lab experience has allowed me to gain knowledge and tools to implement this new practice in a meaningful way for my second graders."

Labs provide a vision of a learning environment and instructional practice to which teachers can strive. Excerpts from a letter that Carrie Symons (who later became a lab teacher herself) wrote to Patrick Allen after her first lab experience in his classroom illustrate the practical breadth and depth of learning that can come from seeing an idea implemented.

January 10, 2001

Dear Patrick,

After the first day of this lab, I walked away exhilarated by the possibilities that await me as a teacher. . . . Here is some of what I observed:

- Critical pedagogical components such as literacy, reading comprehension, writing, critical thinking, problem solving, and community building are neatly woven together in your reader's and writer's workshops.
- Your sense of community reveals itself in class discussions, in the way students choose partners with ease, in the way that they listen to one another and make choices to stay focused on what is being learned and taught.
- You have created a space in which it is safe to ask questions and seek answers.
- Your students have stamina for long periods of reading and writing.
- You are the model for your behavioral expectations.

Now it is up to me to come to terms with what I've seen. I have questions. . . . It's not going to look like your classroom and it shouldn't. But can mine be as successful as yours? Can I teach it as well as you can?

It takes courage to grow. It takes courage to fail. And it takes time to craft the art of teaching the way you have, Patrick.

Thank you for opening the doors to your classroom. Now I am convinced that teaching is art.

Sincerely,

Carrie Symons

I have heard more than one teacher say, "I want to be a Carole Quinby." When I ask, "What about Carole Quinby do you like?" they first respond with concrete details of her teaching expertise such as the arrangements in the physical environment. Jahnell Periera, seventh-grade language arts teacher at Prairie Middle School, recalled, "I remember the environment in Carole Quinby's classroom, the books are everywhere and easily accessible to the students. I ran out and got books so there will be tons of books for years to come in the language arts classroom. I want to organize them the way Carole did—like a little library so the students learn how to find what they want."

The specific environment and classroom arrangements as seen in the context of concrete examples of Carole's practice are made more meaningful when observers are aware that her every action is infused with a deep love and respect for the children's capacity.

Structures and Logistics: A minimum of three to four visits per year, although there have been labs that were offered once a month for a whole year or for two days in a one-week time frame.

The quality of the experience for visiting teachers relies primarily on the demonstrating lab teacher's skill and capacity. A profile of an effective lab teacher would include certain aspects of experience, understanding, disposition, and ability:

- depth of experience in what is to be demonstrated
- well-developed understanding of the theoretical underpinnings of the instructional approach and strategies
- disposition for continually wondering and striving for further learning
- ability to teach children and also articulate the process to adults

Labs are most successful for participants when the classroom teacher explicitly describes:

- long-term goals
- specific strategies to meet those goals
- general information about the students' needs and strengths
- ongoing questions, challenges, adjustments, and adaptations

Sometimes observers don't realize all the thought and detailed planning that precede what they saw occur between the teacher and students. In order to make this visible to observers, the facilitator and lab teacher are in close contact before the lab to discuss the instructional focus, what the teacher is planning to do and hoping to accomplish. In some situations, especially with a first-time lab teacher, the facilitator may offer support to the teacher in developing plans for the lessons to be observed. It is crucial that observing teachers take note not only of the teaching but also know the thinking and planning behind it.

When I first worked as a facilitator in Carrie Symons' fifth-grade lab classroom, she and I communicated via email and by phone as well as in person for at least two weeks before the actual lab. She wrote to me with her initial thinking about the students' needs, and we discussed what we thought would be helpful for the participants to see. Her emails offered a glimpse into the big picture she uses to develop plans that both meet the needs of her students and provide a demonstration of teaching strategies and approaches.

> I'll be heading into synthesis, using *Encounter* by Jane Yolen. I'll also be using other texts to supplement that have different perspectives of Columbus.
>
> For the social studies content standard—Point of View—I want students to understand that history is simply stories written from a variety of perspectives.
>
> In addition, we'll be working on writing two-paragraph book reviews for self-selected texts and hitting some necessary Colorado State Assessment Performance skills such as summarizing, pulling out characters, main events. And then include a persuasive paragraph about whether or not the reader liked the book and why. Would they recommend it?
>
> For writing, I was also thinking of using Jane Yolen as a mentor author, looking at her craft. But my overall goal is to have them write a persuasive essay on whether or not Christopher Columbus was a villain or a hero.

So that's the overall plan. Can you help me figure out what to do when?

Thanks so much,

Carrie

From this initial communication, Carrie and I continued an email, phone, and coffee shop conversation refining the focus and articulating the purpose of what students would learn and observers would see—synthesis and persuasive writing. After we had worked together a few times and she had completed her first year of opening up her classroom for labs and visits, she figured out her own steps for planning and only occasionally asked for further support in clarifying and developing her ideas.

Facilitation

Before the observation, participants arrive early enough so the following can occur:

1. Participants walk around the room and note the physical environment, arrangements of furniture, wall charts, displays of student work, book and materials organization, etc.
2. At the first meeting, participants share prior experience/ background knowledge related to the day's observation. At subsequent meetings, participants share what they have tried in their classrooms and/or what they have been thinking about or wondering since the last observation.
3. Participants respond to the question When you leave today, what would you like to have learned?
4. Participants articulate current questions or challenges.
5. The teacher describes what he will be doing that day— goals for students' learning and understanding, background of students and what they have been working on in the classroom; current question or challenges.

6. The teacher provides preliminary answers to questions that participants have posed.
7. The group pauses before students arrive.

During the Observation

Teacher-participants observe and take notes on what they see. Taking notes provides an important record of observations and thinking for later discussion and reflection as well as for future reference. To scaffold and record thoughts along with observing, double-entry columns are a useful way to organize notes. Participants record scripted observations in the left column—what happened, what was said—and in the right column they record thinking, questions, reactions, or other thoughts directed toward a particular focus such as connections to one's own practice, inferred beliefs underlying the teacher's choice of activity, or a response to the lab teacher's focus question.

If we are observing for a whole morning, I offer an option of debriefing in the hallway at the midway point as a chance to get everyone's initial burning thoughts expressed. Individuals are also encouraged to go into the hallway if they have thoughts or questions to address at any point during the observation. Setting clear boundaries to the silent observer role protects the integrity of the classroom and the children's experience while also respecting each adult learner's individual learning style.

After the Observation

Nearly all teachers report that their most powerful learning occurs during collegial discussion after an observation, with an initial focus on:

- learning that occurred for students;
- explicit strategies the teacher used; and
- how the teacher's intentions were carried out.

Immediately following the observation, participants take a few minutes to look over their entries, noting what they particularly want to discuss or question as well as ideas related to the focus the facilitator has identified for them.

Since labs include more than one session and participants' needs change with each subsequent observation, I have developed a sequence that scaffolds thinking to construct increasingly meaningful understanding and new ideas. The following model is designed for four sessions but could be adapted.

When possible, write these headings on a piece of chart paper and record participants' items of discussion so they can see their thinking.

Session One: The purpose is to help participants begin to develop a schema within which to hold the details of the instructional activities they have observed. These discussions are structured so that each person is given a chance to respond (see Figure 4–4).

1. Describe one thing you saw and/or heard.
2. What threads or commonalities do you see through these descriptions?
3. What questions do you have?
4. Ask questions of the lab teacher and listen to her thinking about what occurred.
5. What will you try in your classroom? What will you continue to ponder?

Session Two: The purpose is to help participants see beyond methods and activities to the underlying thinking and beliefs that are at the core of making the instruction effective. I use a sequence that Sam Bennett developed (see Figure 4–5 on page 64).

1. Describe briefly one thing you saw or heard.
2. Share a favorite moment.
3. List all teaching strategies used.
4. Choose one strategy to look at in more depth. Discuss why this is more than a "tip or trick," more than just another activity.
5. Talk about the belief(s) underlying the use of this strategy.
6. What are you thinking about for your own practice? What new idea will you try or explore?

Observation Debrief I

Purpose is to help participants begin to develop a schema within which to hold the details of the instructional activities that they have observed.

Observation	Questions	Threads	Application

Figure 4–4: *Record Responses to Debrief Questions on a Chart*

Observation Debrief II

Purpose is to help participants see beyond methods and activities to the underlying thinking and beliefs that are at the core of making the instruction effective.

Observation	Favorite Moment	Strategies	Belief	Application

Figure 4-5: *Record Responses to Debrief Questions on a Chart*

Session Three: The purpose is to focus on student learning and performance as a source of information to inform instruction.

1. Use a structure or protocol to look at student work, preferably a sample from a lesson that was observed.
2. What will you try in your classroom or school building? What might you share with colleagues?

Session Four: The purpose is to identify implications for practice and continued exploration—to solidify the application of learning. At the end, the facilitator asks the essential questions that ensure follow-through and application and teachers respond in writing as well as verbally (see Figure 4–6).

In-house labs

Description: Labs offered by teachers to colleagues in their own building. Teachers open their classrooms for formalized observations with a particular instructional focus. This kind of sharing can occur when there is at least a minimal level of trust among faculty members.

Purpose: In some schools, teachers with particular skills provide demonstrations on a regular basis over a period of time and thus help the school community build momentum and independently sustain change. At other schools, when teachers discover something new or after they have attended a lab at another school, they may invite colleagues to see what they are doing and thus spread the benefit of the learning. This is a highly collegial activity that guides teachers to learn from each other, not necessarily to show perfection or expertise, but rather as an invitation to colleagues to join in exploring best practice for the students. In-house labs can build, or build on, a relationship of learning from each other. They can consist of one teacher observing another or a whole group finding the time to observe together.

Structure: Careful and sensitive facilitation and support is especially crucial for teachers offering a demonstration for their own colleagues. It is helpful to follow the same formal

Final Reflection

The purpose of this final reflection is to identify new thinking and changes in practice that have occurred as a result of the lab experience.

What new thinking about teaching will you carry back with you to your classroom?

What will you do differently with your students?

How will you share this new thinking and practice with colleagues?

Figure 4–6: *Written and Verbal Responses to These Essential Questions Can Also Serve as An Evaluation of the Learning Experience*

structure as for either demonstration lessons or out-of-school labs. To ensure that observing teachers are aware of the planning, watch a demonstration and debrief them as soon after the lesson as is possible. A clear structure that aims feedback at what can be learned rather than evaluating the teacher or the students is most helpful. Or, a colleague or coach might offer to help the lab teacher plan or even to co-teach to minimize exposure to initial judgment as norms for these observations become established.

In-house labs can serve many purposes. Anne Goudvis asks experienced teachers to offer in-house labs as a way to introduce new teachers to particular instructional strategies or approaches. When Anne and I began our first year as staff developers at Aspen Creek, some of the teachers had already worked with PEBC in previous buildings and had been using their learning in the classroom. The administrators arranged for teams of teachers to be released from the classroom and Debbie Deem, the literacy specialist, provided support for the brave volunteer lab teachers in their planning. After each one-hour observation, teams debriefed and planned with Debbie, Anne, and I for how they would use what they had learned in their observations.

At the beginning of the last year with PEBC staff development, teachers at Foster Elementary decided to organize their own demonstration lessons for each other as a way to independently sustain their ongoing growth as professionals. Teachers volunteered to demonstrate in their classrooms, and a schedule was organized that didn't call for substitute teachers, but took place during planning time and lunch breaks, so everyone could participate. After the first round of observations, they learned that a formalized facilitated debrief with time specifically set aside was critical to getting the most learning out of the experience, both for the demonstrating teacher and for observers.

After two years of intensive conversation and coaching, science teacher Jeff Cazier and language arts teacher Tim

Reyes opened their classrooms at Prairie Middle School to colleagues. They did this, not with the idea that they were experts showing what should be done but rather with a clearly stated offer to show others what they were discovering and accomplishing with their students. Twelve teachers chose to meet during their planning time as well as before and after school in order to observe and talk.

Sam Bennett and I provided formal facilitation for a thirty-minute prebrief before school started, for ninety-minute observations offered in both morning and afternoon classes, and for the forty-five-minute debrief after school. Structures used for regular labs were adapted to the shorter time frame for these in-house labs. The common observations allowed for a collegial discussion about what is most important in teaching the children, and what the participants, as teachers, could do to ensure motivation and possibilities for success.

The willingness of teachers to risk demonstrating for colleagues requires that a coach or partner ensures a level of trust and safety through sensitive facilitation, clear structures, and preparation. The willingness of observing teachers to learn from colleagues also requires a level of trust and a common assumption about the value and benefit of continual and mutual learning. This sets a precedent for collaborative learning and team building that helps sustain an instructional approach within the school communities.

One-Time School Visits

Description: A team, or even the whole school faculty, leaves the home building for a one-time visit to another classroom or school where particular elements of instructional practice can be seen and experienced.

Purpose: Getting out of the building together often helps groups of teachers think more openly about possibilities. This can help them clarify, expand, and even build a picture of where they are going. The collective experience serves as an anchor for subsequent discussions and reflections about current practice and possibilities. While the visits are most often to see exemplary models of instructional practice, visits can be made to see individual teachers or teams of teachers or whole faculties who are involved in a focus that is of interest to another particular school faculty. Through seeing the process in developmental steps as well as seeing the reality of achievement, visitors learn how to meet their goals.

Structures and Logistics: The process usually starts with a conversation between the principal, a group of teachers and (whenever applicable) a coach or staff developer to identify what would be most valuable to see at another school. It is crucial to have someone designated as a facilitator for the visit— for the initial contacts and arrangements, observations, and discussion afterward. When the population, grade level, or school context is very different from the visitor's situation, a facilitator is especially needed to help visitors see the essential elements and strategies that transfer to their situation. A district coach, teacher-leader, or administrator can fulfill this role.

Many schools use district inservice days for these visits and then, in the afternoon, everyone returns to school or meets for lunch to debrief and discuss implications for their school and practice. The rest of the structure is similar to that of a regular lab, with discussion and focus before the observation, a full debrief after, and perhaps more immediate emphasis on the implications for practice and change both in individual classrooms and in the whole school.

School visits help teachers see how all the various pieces eventually come together. After a couple of months of demonstration lessons and faculty inservices at Witt Elementary School, the teachers were struggling to understand where they were going. With an inservice day approaching, a visit to provide a concrete experience seemed like a good idea. A large group of teachers visited classrooms at Foster Elementary School, which is in the same district but in a very different neighborhood. Several teachers, who were familiar with the history of Foster from years past, were immediately struck that the school was different than they expected.

With a facilitator for each grade-level group, the visitors observed in classrooms. At first, they hurriedly wrote down ideas for creating classroom environments and showing student work, such as charts of children's thinking and displays of student writing as well as math work, all illuminated by white holiday lights along fifth–sixth-grade teacher Mary Young's walls.

Walking out of a classroom, sixth-grade teacher Leon Vasquez whispered to me, "Now we know it isn't just pie in the sky. It can be done." After listening to teachers at Foster relate their stories of challenges and successes, the Witt teachers knew that their struggles did not mean they were doomed. Comments followed such as, "If they can do it with their students, we can certainly do it with our students." "I want our school to feel like this." They discussed what was possible for them individually and in teams, what this vision could do for their students and for the school community as a whole.

When I arrived one morning a week after the visit, Leon ran up to me, "I have a new religion!" he exclaimed. I looked at him warily, expecting he had found a new focus or program that wouldn't leave time for our work together. "Math notebooks," he whispered. In the fifth–sixth-grade classroom at Foster, he had seen students using math notebooks to explain their thinking and record their learning. When he brought this idea into his classroom, his students were immediately excited to be in regular dialogue on an individual basis with their teacher. This communication motivated them to work more systematically on their math lessons. Leon was excited because he had ongoing assessment of the students' understanding to inform his teaching. His excitement spread to other teachers, who also began to effectively use math journals with their students.

Practice: Learning from Experience

"My learning curve is like a rocket, a straight line up."

—Susan McIver, teacher,
Little Elementary School

Susan McIver, a first-grade teacher, has been a model of the willingness to continually and actively dive into deep waters in order to learn. She has steadily refined and extended her teaching practice as a Title One teacher by working with other classroom teachers in trying new methods by exploring new ways of reading and writing for herself, and most recently, as a lab teacher by presenting in front of others in her own classroom. It is in taking the leap into practice, with background knowledge built from observations, reading, and conversation that the most dramatic shifts and jumps in understanding occur.

For teachers, there are two primary ways to practice new instructional strategies.

Teacher as Student

It is through our own experience in reading—using these strategies very consciously at times—that we internalize and are able to teach them. (Keene and Zimmermann 1997)

Patrick Allen, a PEBC staff developer and lab teacher, once related his experience as a swim instructor during his adolescent years when he realized that to teach children how to swim, he couldn't stay on the side of the pool telling them about it. He had to get in the water with them, and model fearlessness by showing them exactly how to do the strokes most effectively. And he had to know how to do the correct strokes in order to teach them.

Since many teachers did not have positive experiences as students themselves, it is crucial that they have new experiences to reverse their negative feelings lest they unintentionally but implicitly convey those to students. Susan McIver recalls that as a beginning reader, "The teacher told me to look at the pictures and always, 'Sound it out! Sound it out!' I was an average reader, not a struggler, never enjoyed it because it was always so hard, but I forced myself." In order to teach comprehension strategies to her students, she says, "I had to figure out the strategies for myself and how I used them because I couldn't teach unless I understood it myself. Now I just go crazy if I don't have a plan for the next book I'm going to read." Susan's new picture of teaching and learning, her passion for books, and for reading and writing, permeate the environment and conversation in her classroom.

Jackie Hockney, a seventh-grade language arts teacher at Base Line Middle School and once-reluctant writer, agreed to write her own short stories as models for her students as part of a writer's workshop. With inspiration from *The World's Shortest Stories* (Moss 1998) ideas for complete stories started coming to her at all times of the day. She happily shared her poetic outpourings with her students. Her joy and satisfaction in writing down all her ideas and having a place for her complex imagination bubbled over in her lessons. She modeled every aspect of the writing process, including how to receive feedback without, as one student worried, having her "feelings hurt," but rather considering the responses of the readers. Her students shared her joy and many of them also began getting ideas at all times of the day. Their interest in and motivation to hone their skills grew as they became excited about what they could express through writing. As teachers, we should be aware of our own struggles with learning, and share our success in overcoming barriers with students.

Practice in the Classroom

At some point, it is time to dive in and try new ideas in the classroom—so there is actual change where it counts. Some teachers may prefer to try new practice on their own, while others will ask for the support of co-teaching with someone who has experience—a staff developer, coach, or fellow teacher.

When teachers start trying out new strategies on their own, they identify and develop their individual styles, preferences, and understanding. They can see what questions arise and what is hard for them to do successfully. Ideally, they gain satisfaction of increased impact on student learning.

After co-teaching with Deanne Davies and Lisa Turner in their sixth-grade language arts classes at Aspen Creek K–8, I was anxious to see what they would do independently the following year. Would they move to the phase of independent practice and application?

Lisa took a position as a literacy resource teacher with a clear vision of what she wanted to bring to that role and to the classrooms in which she would be working. Anne Goudvis and I supported her in planning for work with students and with teachers throughout the year. In this role and with the trust and knowledge of each other that had developed the previous year, we helped her introduce concepts and activities.

Deanne began her year with a classroom structure based on elements of writer's workshop from the previous year's experience. When she told me about how her first weeks were going, her eyes gleamed with excitement. The students were absorbed in their writing and she was teaching them needed skills to create satisfactory narratives and reports within a context of choice and high standards. She was able to use sequences and structures we had developed together, along with Lisa, Debbie, and Caroline, the year before. Whenever we talked about the challenges she still faced, I would say, "Do you want me to come in?" She would often reply, "I don't want to take all your time and I think I can do it on my own." All she still asked was that I be available to discuss ideas and questions. Deanne found a way to continually push the edges of her own practice; she has since become a lab teacher, opening her classroom to visitors from other schools, able to speak eloquently of her purpose, goals, and strategies for guiding students in becoming engaged skillful readers and writers.

When trying new methods and approaches together, teams or the whole faculty can provide each other with both moral and material support while also building their capacity for collaboration. Whenever I see a great teacher, I see a person who loves to do what she is asking or offering the students. Helping teachers find excitement and joy in reading, writing, math, science, or research through learning skills and finding personal meaning means opening the door to their own possibilities for greatness.

Chapter 5

Reflections on Practice

We listened to each other's voices.

—Andrea Holten, third-grade teacher,
Foster Elementary School

Guiding Questions

What times are scheduled when faculty or teams are together?
How could these times be organized to allow for focused discussion on teaching and learning?
Which individuals and groups need more opportunity to talk with each other?
What agreements and structures would be useful to ensure constructive productive use of time together?
What topics and questions are at the top of your list for discussion?

*T*eachers often say they are especially thankful that the presence of a staff developer, coach, or committed principal ensures that time will be set aside for them to talk with each other about their work. Robert Garmston and Bruce Wellman wrote that supporting collegial discussions "may be the most significant investment faculties can make for student learning" (1998).

Professional development need not mean only listening to an expert present information. It can be discovery through various collaborative exploratory processes. While witnessing or participating in the same event, each person actually sees through his unique lens of perspective, background, and questions.

Respecting and valuing these differences brings new thoughts to each of us and helps form profound working relationships.

Carolyn Abey, principal at Foster Elementary, observed, "The best move I made as a leader was to allow release time for people to sit down and say this is where we need to go and this is what we're going to do and I'll assume responsibility of this or I'll assume responsibility for that. . . . Not only did the teachers take responsibility, but they also took ownership and leadership for the plan."

Using every possible opportunity for teachers to share their experiences, questions, and expertise enriches and broadens collective understanding, learning, and determination.

Planning Conversations

Masterful teachers often make their classroom work look effortless. The hours of planning and hard thinking are not necessarily evident from classroom observations. Meeting with teachers as they develop their plans is an important way for a staff developer to inform teacher practice.

Carefully planning and intentionally organizing these meetings yields powerful concrete results. It is often helpful if the teachers have a structure to guide their thinking and planning in these meetings (see Figure 5–1).

Asking questions, making suggestions, and facilitating problem solving provide scaffolding to consider new ideas in both process and content.

- Ask questions that lead to identifying purpose, such as: What is the learning you want the students to come away with at the end of this lesson?
- Offer suggestions of new strategies and activities to promote thoughtful, engaged learning.
- Facilitate problem solving, such as how to adapt a lesson to meet the range of students' abilities and needs.

**Questions to Consider in Preparation
for a Planning Meeting**

1. What support and information do you need to effectively teach this strategy (skill, content, or concept)?

2. What resources does your team need?

3. What are special needs of individual students? Who are those students needing special intervention?

4. How can you implement this strategy in reading, writing, math, research, and the arts?

Figure 5–1: *Questions to Consider in Preparation for a Planning Meeting*

For planning specific lessons, an agenda to take the teacher(s) through a sequential thinking process is helpful.

- Talk about what you have already done.
- Identify what needs to be done—concerns, gaps, and goals.
- Brainstorm how to address concerns, gaps, and goals.
- Plan specific detailed instructional steps with a time frame and responsibilities outlined.

At the beginning of the first year at Prairie, Sam and I gave the teachers the following list to help them maintain a clear focus for planning instruction:

Determine Goals

- Determine what goals are essential for student learning. What do you need to cover (teach)?
- Develop a model of instruction that meets those learning goals. What will the students get (learn)?

Address the Focus

- What is the clear objective that will capture learning for that day?
- Articulate the explicit purpose for each activity you provide for students.
- How will you connect the students to what they're doing?
- Consider the amount of time needed to adequately complete learning.
- Is it possible to do less to get more?

Application

- Focus Questions: Listen to the students' questions. Find a way to record their thinking and questions that cannot be addressed in that moment.
- Model your thinking and provide a scaffold for release of responsibility to independent practice. How much modeling do the students still need? How will it be modeled?

- Ask students to articulate their process: How did you get that answer? What made you think that? Where in the text did that thought (or question) come to your mind?
- Establish and commit to routines, rituals, and procedures that are predictable and that give students ownership of their time. Don't make them wait to hear each next step from the teacher.
- Plan time every day for reading, writing, and thinking.

Reflection

- Who is doing most of the work here?
- What did the students take with them from today's class?
- What evidence do I have that we achieved today's goal(s)?

Frameworks to support focused reflection and conversation about what is most important in planning for student learning provide tools that teachers can use independently. With repeated experience in focused planning, habits of thought and approach are established for independent application of new ideas.

Debriefing Sessions

The debrief (described in more detail in Chapter 4) is the chance to synthesize and transfer learning from an experience to implications or plans for practice. After teaching or observing, a focused discussion cements and expands the new insights and ideas and gives depth and dimension to the observation. When a lesson has gone well, it is crucial that the elements for success on the part of the teacher are identified in such a way that they could be replicated. Lessons that don't go well are often a great opportunity to learn, as the group identifies all the dynamics and elements that led the plan astray. Lessons from those inevitable times can be most profound when used as a springboard.

The debrief is also an opportunity to learn more about one's colleagues, their beliefs, and their knowledge about students and learning. Through discussion of observed instruction, teachers recognize common values or surprising insights, lean on each other for outside perspectives and differing points of view. The experience of each person in a school building is enriched, and complex relationships based on knowledge of each other's thinking are developed.

Study Groups

Study groups are designed for participants to gain and develop new thinking and knowledge in a rigorous collaborative context of a professional learning community.

Study groups are usually voluntary unless they are held during regular faculty meeting times. Principals or staff developers often can arrange for teachers to receive either continuing education or university credit for their participation. Sometimes teacher aides, parents, or teachers from other schools are included. It is helpful to have a facilitator to keep everyone focused. In the beginning, the group might ask a coach or staff developer to facilitate until their norms and routines are well established.

The steps to establishing a study group include:

- Identify a focus for collaborative study.
- Identify text(s) for professional learning.
- Identify how the meeting will be structured and facilitated.

Any goal for gaining knowledge, skill, and understanding can be fruitful for group study. When participants meet in a study group, they may discuss the content of a text as well as their own processes of making meaning and comprehending the ideas and information.

Groups may choose to focus on a particular question or idea and investigate it through a variety of readings such as professional books or articles reflecting the most current research, novels, or other nonfiction texts. Videos of classroom teachers can also serve as text sources for inquiry and discussion.

Groups who want to learn about teaching a particular strategy or skill to students may choose to explore their own processes in that area. As they experience the dynamics and benefits as well as challenges of using a particular strategy, they begin to develop an understanding of what is involved and what they will need to support their students.

Teachers may also choose to look at a particular subject or skill such as mathematical problem solving, the research process in science or social studies, or aspects of the writing process. Nonfiction trade books that address a topical issue pertinent to classroom themes can serve as a rich source for discussion and professional learning.

People from different schools who share an interest or role have also formed study groups. In Boulder, Colorado, three middle school principals started a study group to which they invited all their colleagues. For the last three years, a core group has continued to meet monthly at each one of their schools. The members of the group developed agendas for these meetings that include:

- Check-in: current issues and concerns or celebrations— limited discussion
- Observation in a classroom or tour of the school: protocol for school walk
- Focused conversation around a particular educational, administrative, or leadership issue
- Reading to support thinking and address questions
- Reflection and conversation. What new thinking or idea for action do I have now? What did we do today that will impact children?
- Plan for next meeting

Members of the group document their thinking and experience in journals during and in between meetings. Formal notes are kept by the facilitator and shared over the Internet. In spite of their overly busy schedules, participants report that because the meetings give them concrete ideas and insight into the bigger picture, they leave revitalized and with a renewed sense of purpose. The chance to talk and learn from valued colleagues, to speak from both the heart and mind, adds to their capacities as leaders. They have also developed a collective vision of doing what is best for the whole community rather than merely their own schools. In the process of meeting over the years, they have gained increasing support from the district and developed a model for professional study that has subsequently been adopted by other groups of administrators.

Faculty Meetings

Faculty meetings, a logical time for teachers to talk with each other, are traditionally used for handling business and disseminating information. With a commitment to improving instruction across the whole school, many principals use these meetings to focus on instructional issues and professional development.

Given the complexities of school priorities and responsibilities, living up to such a commitment can present a serious challenge. Many times, I have watched and waited after someone informed me, "I just have one quick announcement before you get started." This often opens the door to either discussion about the announcement or another quick announcement that just has to be made then. The minutes go by and, finally, I get my chance to rush through the "focus on instruction."

As a staff developer, I have at times provided support, motivation, and even applied pressure on the principal to regulate how time is used in meetings. Because I have both struggled with this issue and seen powerful results from successfully addressing it, I have learned to ask this question of anyone who is considering taking this time: Is this information more important than learning about instruction? Could it be communicated equally effectively in another way such as email or voice mail? Predictable structures that teachers can rely on help maintain a time commitment. People become accustomed to the rituals and routines if they are assured work will be accomplished, everyone's voice will be heard, and the time will be of value to their immediate instructional needs. When they have experienced this value, they come to share responsibility for how time is used.

Structures to ensure that faculty meetings are devoted to instructional discussion can include:

- Having a representative group meet regularly to discuss business and make recommendations for the whole faculty's approval.
- Delivering information about business from the principal via voice and email in a succinct and concise format.
- Rotating teacher responsibility for faculty meetings that focus on teaching and learning. In these meetings, designated facilitators decide on a theme for the meeting. They might present a project or lesson that has gone well, take their colleagues through a particular strategy lesson, share samples of student work, or bring an article for everyone to read and discuss in regard to process or content and implications for the classroom.
- Committing time during faculty meetings for teachers to share successes so that other teachers might hear of new effective instructional strategies and activities. An unintended consequence of this time is an increased respect for colleagues who take risks to improve the efficacy of their instruction.

Teachers often request time to meet with colleagues from other grade levels during faculty meetings. This provides an opportunity they cannot find anywhere else in the school schedule and is important for establishing common ground for all students, sharing goals and strategies, and brainstorming ways to support each other in younger children's preparation and in older children's developmental continuity. I have seen these ongoing meetings build a much more cohesive community whose support for students crosses traditional boundaries.

Each of these small steps contributes to a schoolwide momentum and promotes change for every teacher and her classroom of students. The faculty's engagement and personal investment in learning becomes evident in their facilitation of conversations around instruction.

Inservices

> I hope when I die it will be during an inservice. . . . It will be a subtle transition from life to death.
>
> —Joke circulating on the Internet

The first challenge when facing teachers on an inservice day is to overcome their expectations from past experiences. The potential for a truly valuable inservice day increases significantly when the facilitator or presenter knows and is known by the participants; has established trust and credibility; and can tailor the session to meet the interests, needs, and strengths of the group of people who have entered the room. This is an ideal situation, however, and cannot be counted on to be the case. One way to cross the chasm between as yet unknown presenters and a school community is to include administrators and representative faculty members in planning and facilitation sessions. Also, conducting these meetings as focused work sessions rather than presentations promotes participation and input from the group. Work sessions are organized around solid structures that allow time for directed formalized content and skill building with longer sessions for exploration, practice, and planning for application. Participants' activity, input, and questions infuse the day. Using the information and expertise of the facilitator, they seek the lessons and meaning that are relevant to them at that time rather than passively receiving, and perhaps rejecting, information merely supplied by others. Most significantly, the inservice day is an opportunity for facilitators to model their ideas of best practice for teaching and learning so that teachers can experience the benefits for themselves (see Figure 5–2).

**Gradual Release of Responsibility Plan
for an Inservice**

Crafting the Lessons

Strategy _____ Date _____

Focus and Purpose: *What is to be learned and why? Key points. Introduction to students*

    Focus:
    Purpose:

Modeling: *What will be demonstrated? Resources, books, and time line*

Guided Practice: *Structure and scaffolding to support strategy exploration. Opportunities for response*

Independent Practice: *Opportunity to use strategy and share struggles and success*

Application and Follow-up: *Experiences to use and revisit skill or strategy*

Notes

———

Figure 5–2: *Gradual Release of Responsibility Plan for an Inservice (adapted from Kristin Venable)*

Range of Approaches

Generally, the same principles and strategies for working with students apply to working with adults. In fact, it is ideal to use the same instructional models or strategies with teachers for their use with students. Teachers can experience the learning methods, which will help them internalize and understand the dynamics that make them work. I use the elements of a workshop model and gradual release of responsibility to structure the learning opportunities along with cognitive strategies to scaffold thinking and build understanding.

The worst inservice I have faced included a lack of knowledge about the group's situation, no food, mandatory attendance, no credibility, and no established trust or relationship. Basically, it was a one-size-fits-all presentation that did not fit the group at all because the decisions about what the teachers needed to "get" were made, probably with the best of intentions, at an administrative level.

There are many gifted presenters who are able to hold and perhaps entertain any audience with their personal charisma and deep knowledge of a particular topic. These kinds of inservices can offer inspiration and encouragement, provoke questions and new thinking, and provide validation and new ideas, but in the long run, have limited impact on what teachers actually transfer to their classrooms. A heavy reliance on the power of the presentation communicates the implicit message that teachers are passive recipients rather than responsible and active participants in their own learning and growth.

A mandatory inservice, whether it includes many schools or one school, must offer choice and respect for participants to voice what they believe they need to learn at that time. This may require that presenters be able to adjust plans on the spot according to what they learn about the participating teachers. If the presenter can articulate how her content relates to current issues and challenges such as teaching to standards, increasing scores on standardized tests, motivating students, or managing the work load for meaningful instruction, she will build credibility and relevant purpose from the beginning.

A common theme heard is "Please don't waste my time. I have so little of it." In most cases, teachers consider time well spent if a balance is struck between presentation of information and offerings of specific ideas for immediate application in their classrooms, with time to think and talk, to make meaning, and to find connections to actual practice. My most basic goal is to plan so that participants leave the room at the end of the day with a clear idea of what they have learned, with new questions to consider, with at least one new idea for the classroom, and with reawakened inspiration.

Structured Conversations and Critical Friends Groups

Many educators have found a powerful tool in using protocols for structured conversations that lead a group through an efficient and intentional process of clarifying and expanding ideas and viewpoints around an issue, student work, or teacher practice. The structure of these discussions provides opportunities for each person to speak and to listen so that, at the end, there is a satisfying sense of whole-group participation and clarity. Following protocols that keep people within agreed-upon norms for productive collegial conversations can alter the dynamics of a school culture.

> A protocol creates a structure that makes it safe to ask challenging questions of each other; it also ensures that there is some equity and parity in terms of how each person's issues are attended to. The presenter has the opportunity not only to reflect on and describe an issue or a dilemma, but also to have interesting questions asked of him or her, and to gain differing perspectives and new insights. Protocols build in a space for listening, and often give people a license to listen without having to continuously respond. (Colorado Critical Friends Group 2002)

Andrea Holten, a third-grade teacher at Foster Elementary School, identified her challenge of "scheduling to allow [her] to incorporate all aspects of sound literacy instruction." Caryl Hawkins recalled that they "started having a great discussion, then fell back into talking about the past, but the protocol brought us back to focus on helping Andrea with her dilemma." Margie Robinson, a Title One teacher at Foster, says when she "presented a dilemma to the group, [I] felt the wagons circling to help and take care of this together."

Most protocols follow a similar timed sequence:

1. Presenter gives a brief, prepared description of the issue, question, or work to be discussed.
2. Participants ask clarifying and probing questions.
3. Participants discuss student work or issue while presenter listens and takes notes.
4. Presenter responds to the discussion and implications for practice.
5. Everyone talks about what did and didn't work in the process.

Numerous variations on this basic sequence have been, and continue to be, developed by those who are using them. An ever-growing list of protocols for these sorts of conversations continues to be developed by educators around the country. (See websites in References.)

When groups commit to using this tool on an ongoing basis with goals of collaborative inquiry, exploration, and problem solving, they might form a Critical Friends Group (CFG). CFGs are

> the product of a simple idea, providing deliberate time and structures to promote adult professional growth that is directly linked to student learning. Each CFG commits to working together on a long-term basis (at least a semester or preferably the school year) toward better student learning. The members gather for at least one two-to-three hour meeting each month, at which they establish and publicly state learning goals for students, help each other think about more productive teaching practices, examine

curriculum and student work, and identify school-culture issues that affect student achievement. As "critical friends," they (ideally) observe one another at work at least monthly and offer feedback in challenging but non-threatening ways. (National School Reform Faculty 2003)

This can truly be a school-based professional development model where the teachers learn to look at their own practice, often through a careful examination of student work, and where they can gather ideas from each other about how to increase their effectiveness. In Colorado, momentum has grown for this form of collaborative professional development, with many variations in how groups form and how they use the protocols and structures.

Ever-expanding variations on the form of these groups, who participates, and how they are sustained have generated these questions:

- Will participation be mandatory or voluntary? Will protocols be incorporated into already established meetings or will a separate and distinct Critical Friends Group be established?
- Who will facilitate? Will facilitation rotate among participants or will one person carry the responsibility?
- Who will participate? Will participation be open to everyone at any time or at the beginning and perhaps at one other time during the year? Will the group be open to teachers only or to anyone in the school community?
- Where will meetings occur? At school? In different classrooms? In one consistent meeting place such as the library?
- When will meetings be held? Will teachers be released from the classroom for this purpose? Will they be held during planning time, faculty meetings, late start, early release, or free time after school?
- Will we have a particular focus to begin?
- How will we assess results for teacher practice and student learning as a consequence of these meetings?

At Base Line Middle School, principal Candy Hyatt knew she wanted to use professional development time provided by a late start every Wednesday morning for teachers to become better informed about learning, instruction, and curriculum by looking at student work.

I introduced the use of protocols in small groups so that the teachers shared responsibility for facilitation from the beginning and so that they would not need to rely on me except for occasional questions about procedure. We used a protocol to discuss an article that Candy had found about student improvement in schools where teachers used protocols to look at student work. Zeke Tiernan, who teaches seventh-grade geography, exclaimed in the debrief, "We are going to have professional discussions to build our professional relationships and community instead of team-building activities that have no relation to our actual work."

After only a few meetings, Candy was able to continue the practice on Wednesday mornings without my assistance. It was important that the teachers understood they didn't have to use a protocol every time but that protocols were a tool to help them focus, wade through challenges, and learn from each other. When science teacher John Rundell was planning a written report for his science class, he brought the plan to his grade-level team. He stated that his goal was to provide a structure to help all his students achieve success on their research reports. More specifically, he was interested in the quality of writing and communication of information rather than a particular number of pages or quantity of information. Suggestions for structures and specific directions for the assignment as well as support with the writing from colleagues in language arts, special education, and English as a second language poured forth. They were able to identify common themes in their concerns for students and related thoughts about teaching. The focused conversation, which took less than fifty minutes, informed and impacted the team's classroom practice.

At Sheridan Middle School, three faculty members trained as Critical Friends Group coaches in a weeklong summer session. In the fall, they set up a structure with their principal's support for monthly collaborative team meetings during an extra planning time. At first, they looked at student work, then moved to include teacher practice and shared reading. These consistent meetings allowed these teachers to explore beliefs and identify what they do, as well as what they could do, to provide consistency and repetition of skills, language, and attitudes for students across subject areas and classrooms. After participating in a discussion about student work presented by a colleague, one of the participating teachers observed, "His problems are our problems, so I can use this with my students who are experiencing the same situation."

In reflections written at the end of each session, teachers thought about the impact of these collegial conversations.

- "I appreciate the opportunity to just wonder and think about student work. I wish we had more time to do this together."
- "I wonder if I would feel defensive if it were my problem. I probably would, but hopefully I could get beyond that and learn."
- "These sessions seem to provide lots of things that motivate me to do more in class."
- "If classes are commonly lectures, how are we expecting the majority of our kids to understand content?"
- "If we can increase our time spent on hands-on learning maybe we do sacrifice quantity, but we are focused on quality learning and proof of understanding."

The point of protocols and Critical Friends Groups is to have an ongoing "in-depth, insightful conversation about teaching and learning" (Colorado Critical Friends Group 2002). The particulars of how the group is formed and sustained, or even what it is named, doesn't seem to matter as long as the goal of collaborative inquiry, exploration, and problem solving in the best interest of the students is critically maintained. (The word *critical* in this context can be taken to mean urgently important, as in "critical care," rather than the harsher definition associated with the term. Some groups prefer to call themselves learning communities, or inquiry or study groups.) As long as the group maintains its commitment to constructive professional conversations around issues central to their work as educators, a shift in their functional identity can occur; they begin to see themselves more and more as a community of capable, skilled professionals and colleagues.

Informal Conversations in the Teacher's Lounge, Hallways, Classroom

Almost at the other end of the spectrum from structured conversations, informal and spontaneous conversations are just as important to the professional culture of a school. Some of the most heartening stories I have ever heard came to me in hallways as teachers rushed past each other. Their words are like poems in their brevity. Just the facts—like the fact that Ricardo read his story to the class and was flooded with his friends' eager questions in both Spanish and English. Or the details of the breakthrough in Summer's understanding of why division is like subtraction. Or the connection of similar themes that Damien made between *The Stranger* and *Song of the Whale*. From these stories of student learning, everyone moves on with more optimism for the next lesson.

If I continue down the hall and into the faculty lounge, I never know what mood I will find. This room sometimes carries a reputation as a place for griping and venting. One new teacher who was always absent at lunchtime said she had been warned in an education class to avoid the teacher's lounge because it would just bring her down. Sadly, she was also cut off from potential collegial support, friendships, particularly helpful in the first year of teaching.

Some school communities have experimented with establishing norms to avoid the kind of conversation that encourages hopelessness and frustration. They may still allow themselves space for venting when necessary but most of the time, they pose questions, ask for help with problem solving, or share anecdotes that are cause for celebration.

I occasionally arrange with teams to debrief or plan during lunch in the lounge. As we engage in this conversation about a particular lesson and plans for follow-up, we often draw in teachers from other teams, some of whom might not have volunteered to use their lunchtime that way but find themselves interested in our exploration.

As a way of getting to know a school culture and individuals, I try at least once to stay in the lounge through the whole lunch period, watching different groups come and go, listening to teachers' unstructured conversation as they hurry to get back and prepare for the rest of their day. I notice how the themes may change and the mood may shift depending on who enters or exits. I take note of who comes in wanting to talk about an instructional issue or a child, who needs to vent, and who wants to talk about anything but work. Many times, this provides me with an opportunity for an informal personal conversation with one or two teachers who have burning issues to discuss or communicate. I recommend this use of time to anyone who is responsible for seeing the big picture in a school.

Through informal conversation, people learn and reveal more about each other and their own values and thoughts. Opportunities for both informal spontaneous interactions as well as structured, tightly focused dialogue between teachers, administrators, and staff developers are essential to deepening productive working relationships.

Chapter 6

Sustaining Progress

It's not what we're teaching. It's what kids are learning.

—Mary Jo Bode, eighth-grade language arts teacher

Guiding Questions

What are two or three long-term goals for professional learning in your school?

What are your specific goals for teacher learning?

What are your specific goals for student learning?

What instruments and methods for assessment do you use?

  Formal

  Informal

What kinds of data do you and can you collect?

For what purposes do you use assessment data?

Who will see the assessment data?

How will accomplishments be sustained?

*J*oy Hood tells me about a teacher whose practice and view of her students completely changed. She became joyful in her teaching and her students became deeply engaged in their learning. But she ends her story with, ". . . then the staff developer left and the teacher went back to her old ways."

I know that story all too well. A teacher with whom I had once worked later reminisced of the classes we taught together, "That was the most successful unit I ever taught." Yet she tells me she is looking forward to finishing the serious work preparing for the state standardized test so she can get back to the "fun stuff." How had we missed helping these teachers see the serious value in continuing this practice on their own throughout the year?

What is the key to learning through professional development in a way that carries forward? How did Deanne and Lisa at Aspen Creek internalize new ways of teaching so that they understood how to use the elements of gradual release of responsibility and a workshop structure, no matter the content or skills? Why does second-grade teacher Lavonne Bird persist on her own in teaching the way she learned several years ago in a lab with Debbie Miller?

If we don't figure out how to sustain each step forward toward best most effective instructional practice, the money and time spent on professional development is basically thrown away. The answer lies in the capacity to gather and present evidence of results for students tied to specific instructional practice—in one word—assessment. With solid assessment practices, teachers are able to recognize what is working for students, and what they should keep doing. With this knowledge, teachers can experience a sense of efficacy and even joy. Otherwise, they have only a vague sense of success, which is neither reassuring nor sufficiently valid to cause them to wholly change or sustain practice. How simple. Yet how challenging.

Assessing Practice

The issues of assessment plague us in education as we strive to identify accurate, reliable methods and instruments as well as appropriate and credible uses of the methods we have in place. We struggle with the high stakes of standardized tests as well as the validity of other assessments.

As an individual teacher, administrator, or staff developer, I know I have to find and articulate evidence about the effect of my efforts. To say with any degree of authority or certainty that my work affects learning, I have to look toward a variety of approaches that create a comprehensive picture for assessment of teacher practice and student learning.

Writing this chapter, I continually wondered how many readers would want to skip it. Would I, as a reader, want to skip it? Could I even stand to write it? Would readers approach it with hope for easier solutions than have yet been found?

Assessment is a topic often avoided, or greeted with groans and sighs. Yet I wonder why we are not more interested and invested in its possibilities. The current negative associations I frequently hear associated with assessment are addressed in this chapter and include the following:

• Assessment can be used for punishment, checking up when the learner is not trusted. Traditionally, it is out of the hands of the involved parties. Teachers and schools are given scores or "grades" based on state-mandated tests.

• Assessment can be a bunch of numbers that don't tell us the true value of the student's work but rather place the individual in a category or level. These numbers can also be misleading when only part of the story is known. For example, many students are not yet sufficiently proficient in English as their second language to understand the language of the test. Without sufficient understanding of English, they are likely to be lost, yet if they don't take the test at all, they are given a score of zero that lowers the school average.

• Assessment is a frustrating topic because we haven't figured out consistently reliable and manageable instruments in the context of large-scale public education to offer meaningful information that can guide instruction. The complexity of what we want to know and the challenge of the logistics can be humbling.

There are also at least as many positive views of the possibilities for assessment:

• Assessment can be a means to get to know the learners, what they are learning, how they learn, and what they need.

• Assessment plans can combine different methods to get complex pictures of the effect or results of our practice. Evidence of effect or results can include test scores and graduation rates, parent participation, and discipline incidents as well as reading inventories, running records, and documentation of student conversation and thinking.

• Assessment plans developed and administered by the involved parties provide instruments that reflect the teaching and priorities set within that classroom or community. When student scores on standardized tests are combined with grades, teacher-developed achievement tests, and student portfolios, the data can provide points of discussion for teams and faculty. Familiarity with the assessment instrument and what it asks of students contributes to establishing some parameters or guidelines for instructional decisions.

• Assessment and analysis of data validate practice and the effect of practice on students, which can lead to increased professional strength. The identified benefits, reported in a way that clearly communicates findings, are useful and so the evaluation guides subsequent professional learning and practice.

In the end, it really isn't a question. If we don't have ways to judge how we are doing, how can we make a case for continuing or changing what we do? What will guide us? A feeling that we like it? A hunch that we are doing something right? Valid assessment can give us the reassurance that we are on a track that can be articulated, advocated for, and sustained. When Mary Jo Bode assesses student work, she is asking the student, "How do I as a teacher know that you got what my hope and goal is for your learning?" Then she asks, "How do I go back and help you get what you didn't yet get?" In this way, assessment leads her instructional decisions, to continue or change course and method.

When the first conversations about a professional development initiative or instructional model or program occur, and goals and purpose are identified, questions need to be addressed about how to track progress toward fulfilling that purpose and those goals—what will be assessed, what data will be gathered, and how will it be interpreted and used? The answers are crucial for determining continued support and direction.

What Will We Assess?

Assessing professional development can be confusing because while the professional development itself is geared toward teacher learning—change in understanding, knowledge, and practice—the actual change that matters is in student learning—student understanding, knowledge, and performance. This requires an evaluation of professional development that occurs on multiple levels and designed from the beginning to assess what may occur sequentially, beginning with change in teacher understanding and knowledge, leading to change in teacher practice, leading to change in student understanding and knowledge, and culminating in student demonstration and application of that understanding and knowledge.

A useful assessment design is based on the intended outcome of the school improvement effort starting with goals for students and working back to what the teachers will need to understand, know, and be able to do to help the students meet those goals.

What Data Will Be the Basis for Assessment?

What and how we assess implies and communicates what is being valued in the initiative for improved instructional efficacy and influences what we work toward. If we assess only teacher change, or if our only measure of student learning is a standardized test, the scope of what can be discovered about teaching and learning is narrowed. On the other hand, if different layers of learning as well as different applications are taken into account, several options for gathering useful data emerge.

Since the course and progress of change can waver as contextual pieces change and shift, a consideration of guiding questions at regular intervals helps maintain a focus on the school's needs.

- What are the benchmarks by which results will be assessed?
- How will purpose and goals be revisited and revised?
- How will progress be continuously assessed?
- How are we going to use the data? How will we ensure adequate time to accurately analyze and discuss implications for practice?
- What is the time frame for expected results? For what period of time will we assess teacher learning and then teacher practice and then the impact on student learning and performance?

A consideration of the options for collecting useful data evokes the continuing debate over quantitative versus qualitative evaluation. This debate is important as an articulation of both positions, yet in practice, is likely to never be resolved because each approach has a use when understood and applied appropriately.

Drawing Useful Conclusions from Data

At the heart of the debate over data collection is a basic disagreement as to what conclusions can credibly be drawn from different types of data and therefore how practice (and even school funding) is impacted. On one side are researchers, educators, and politicians who insist that there is hard objective data provided by numbers that give a factual, not interpretive, picture from which to base decisions about educational plans and funding. On another side are those who insist the possible variables that affect an individual student's particular response to a specific item on a given test and day are actually immeasurable. This begs the question of what useful meaning can be drawn from any one particular measure of student learning.

In practice, most educators collect some data that is measurable and concrete and some that is descriptive. Full knowledge of the limits and value of any one type of instrument or measure is crucial to the analysis and application of the information gained. As with other debates in the field of education, the complexity and multiplicity of our charge as educators must lead to the use of a multiplicity of measures, including quantitative and qualitative information.

Combining observations of teacher practice that reflect learning from a professional development model with student data (possibly from standardized tests, reading inventories, and teacher records) yields essentially relevant, useful information to assess the impact of that model.

Data collected to create this multilayered view could include:

- descriptions of instructional strategies or models that the teacher learned and tried in the classroom;
- observation and artifacts from teacher lesson;
- collected anecdotal records, observations, student work samples; and
- standardized tests, reading inventories, and rubric-scored samples of student work.

Some of the data collection will be formative, that is, tracking ongoing progress for continual improvement of the professional development plan. This type of data collection helps ensure that each professional development program meets the participants' needs and expectations, is a meaningful experience, and can be translated into action in the classroom. Some staff developers and administrators use formative evaluation on a daily basis.

Concluding information at the end of a designated time frame about the overall effectiveness of a particular change initiative is obtained for a summative evaluation. Educator practice, organizational change, and student outcomes are three levels for collection of this data and will inform subsequent revisions of the program, steps, and commitments.

In practice, the goals and purposes of the evaluation determine the appropriate evaluation tools or methodology. For example, a survey can take a quantitative approach if its purpose is to measure and predict, or a qualitative approach if its purpose is to understand the dynamics of a developing learning community.

At both the classroom and whole school level, clear goals and an articulation of methods for continual assessment help individuals and communities stay on the course they have set for themselves to reach their desired destination. This is the realm over which professionals in schools have some authority and influence.

Assessing Change in Teacher Understanding and Practice

The change in teacher understanding, beliefs, and practice would, naturally, be the first change to be noted. It is helpful if teachers initially define their hopes for professional development in the specific context and situation. Articulating desired outcomes will lead to appropriate assessment decisions. Among these decisions is a determination as to the type of data that will be most informative. Surveys and observations, notes from meetings, interviews, and staff developer journals can be completed as narratives or as checklists depending on whether the school desires narrative descriptive or numerical quantitative data.

Becoming informed about professional development possibilities through reading current literature about best practice is a starting point to identify purpose and goals. Dennis Sparks and Susan Loucks-Horsley, in *Five Models of Staff Development for Teachers*, wrote, "staff development is defined as those processes that improve the job-related knowledge, skills, or attitudes of school employees" (1990).

More specifically, Judith Warren Little writes, "School faculty set criteria such as whether the proposal reduces teacher isolation, strengthens teachers' capacity to examine and assess their own work, engages teachers in active intellectual activity, and explicitly takes into account their particular school characteristics."

Similarly, the National Staff Development Council (NSDC) has developed standards for best practice staff development. Their standards are divided into context, process, and content categories tied explicitly to the ultimate purpose of improving the learning of all students.

Teachers can check their progress by reviewing their own written and spoken reflections. Staff developers keep written records of observations and meetings to track and document teacher learning and change in practice.

At Prairie Middle School, Sam and I devoted considerable time to observations of teachers and students in the classrooms. Knowing their concerns, challenges, and goals and keeping the areas of focus we had discussed in mind, we could record evidence as they implemented identified practices.

Early in our second year, we observed in each of the classrooms of teachers with whom we worked and recorded common threads:

- Classroom structures: Students move back and forth from whole-group mini-lessons and directions to working individually, in pairs, and in small groups. When students are working, teachers circulate and often confer with individuals. The tasks usually call for students to collaborate. Students have many opportunities to talk with the teacher and with each other.
- Time: The block time is used as an opportunity to develop concepts in learning rather than as isolated chunks of learning as it had been last year. Teachers allowed time for students to think and talk about the work they were completing.
- Cognitive strategies: When giving an assignment, teachers name the kind of thinking the students need to use. Teachers provide or remind students of background knowledge to support task completion or to evoke connections to personal experience that build understanding

of a new concept. Teachers continually ask students: How did you think of that? Why do you think that?

- Classroom environment and relationships: All questions are welcomed and honored. Teachers pause to think about and respond to questions, not necessarily with the answer. Different entry points for learning are provided. The tone is noncoercive—teachers' voices are calm and slow, not rushed and tight. Students step in to help when others are struggling. Teachers place themselves in available spots in the classroom as students tend to linger to talk with them; neither teachers nor students appear anxious to leave the room at the end of class.

In this instance, the priorities for teacher change in "job-related knowledge, skills, or attitudes" had been clearly identified so there was a clear framework for observations that assess and articulate progress. The next step was to identify observable change in students.

Assessing Change in Student Understanding and Performance

Results-driven education for students will require results-driven staff development for educators. Staff development's success will be judged primarily not by how many teachers and administrators participate in staff development programs or how they perceive its value, but by whether it alters instructional behavior in a way that benefits students. (Sparks 1994)

Inseparable yet necessarily separated—teacher and student learning are simultaneously observed and documented so that possible correlations, perhaps even cause and effect, can be identified. Working backward from articulated goals for student learning to necessary teacher knowledge and practice acknowledges the interconnectedness of the dynamic. Stated simply, while professional development focuses on change in teachers' knowledge and practice, improvement in student learning as a consequence of the change in instruction is what ultimately matters.

Questions that arise from the initial articulation of desired goals for student learning and that may guide data collection include:

- How are students thinking? How are students showing their thinking?
- Are students transferring strategies for learning to other areas of curriculum without prompting?
- Are students having focused conversations about the meanings in their books?
- Are students working hard to understand difficult texts or problems? Are they listening to each other's thinking and building on that rather than just moving to their unconnected next thought?
- Do students use writing to express what is important to them? To record what they want to remember?
- Do students understand and remember content and skills from one day to the next?
- Do students have ideas of what to do when they are stuck or challenged?

In order to gauge progress, it is necessary to document the answers to these questions over time. Journals with headings, or notebooks containing all documents and notes, interviews, surveys, and questionnaires are useful tools for this purpose. Pre- and posttests and rubrics providing more categorical types of information can round out the view provided by the more descriptive data.

The two most basic questions to ask are:

1. What are students learning and able to show knowledge of?
2. Where do students still need help?

In addition to mandated tests and formalized inventories, ongoing evaluation with immediate response is possible on an individual teacher/classroom/student level. When a teacher identifies a learning goal that is not being met, she identifies the next step for individual professional development specifically tied to a particular student need.

When Tim Reyes at Prairie Middle School talks about his students, what they need, and what he is trying to provide, he asks specific, targeted questions about observable student performance. One afternoon, he described a group of five students whose handwriting is illegible. He worried that scorers on the state test would be unable to read what the student's wrote when scoring content. He was searching for information about helping middle school–aged students with handwriting skills so that their writing scores wouldn't end up reflecting penmanship rather than actual writing ability. In the same conversation, he identified an ongoing concern about providing adequate challenge and rigor for the students in his advanced class. Tim observes and formally records student work and engagement and then goes in search of resources—books, articles, other teachers' ideas—to help him plan a response within his classroom lesson plans.

A fifth-grade teacher told me her students "just weren't getting" conventions in their writing. She showed me the writing samples and we agreed that many of them were imaginative and had strong voices, but the basic conventions of punctuation around dialogue, complete sentences, and paragraphs were so lacking that the reader had to work too hard. I asked if I could try working with one of the students. I took him into the hall with his fantasy story in hand. Working one-on-one, he helped me navigate the action in his story. I could see the great strength of his narrative voice as well as his conceptual grasp of the fantasy genre. We chose two areas of skill—paragraphs and punctuation for dialogue—to help him communicate his imaginative ideas. I modeled the thinking behind the skills for him and allowed him time to figure it out. His story began to take shape. He wanted to stay longer when it was time for lunch. So did I.

Later, the teacher and I discussed the work of this student and I identified the next step to take with the whole class. I offered her ideas for instruction, and we developed a co-teaching plan to integrate specific conventions within the students' creative expressions to strengthen their writing.

Opportunities for teachers to hear children express their thinking are invaluable in tracking what students are internalizing. Susan McIver describes a book talk on *Journey to Freedom: A Story of the Underground Railroad* by Courtni C. Wright in Barb McAllister's second-grade classroom. The teachers talked about their thinking and at first "nobody was saying anything. Then one student said, 'This is how I see it. These people weren't asked, and they got to America, couldn't do their own thing and it's like they kind of died.' He's going to remember the Underground Railroad and Harriet Tubman . . . talking about books and getting students to talk about these books so they can think about them in a certain way that they're going to remember them forever. Those students will go back to books we read in the beginning of first grade and they haven't forgotten."

Progress toward overarching goals is also important to monitor. Andrea Holten held a goal in mind for her students and watched for evidence. "From the beginning, we had discussions concerning students' voices being heard. A lot of them don't have that chance at home or the power that comes with being heard in their lives." Andrea decided this instructional model was really working when she began to hear students expressing their own thinking. She says, "We were able to come back as a staff to start talking about it, with specific examples from our classrooms, and I think that it changed how we saw the students and allowed us to talk about this goal as a whole staff."

From the very specific to the very general, assessment involves the most important questions:

- What are we teaching?
- What is being learned?
- How do we know?
- What are we going to do about it?

Asset Map: A Structure to Create a Comprehensive Picture for Assessment

The asset mapping process was developed by Ellin Keene along with other PEBC staff developers and school instructional leaders as a tool for ongoing assessment and planning. Using a format originally developed to identify existing strengths in urban and rural communities, Ellin and her colleagues referenced data from research on successful schools to create a list of criteria. From this list, faculty groups could identify their existing strengths and areas of need, initiate conversations, and plan for the specific direction of schoolwide professional development and instructional improvement.

From the discussion, two or three goals are identified and placed on another asset map used to record evidence from multiple sources that show progress toward meeting the goals. This process, especially if undertaken early in the school year, yields valuable information to guide the design of a professional development plan tailored to the school's context.

In each school, the process is often adjusted to meet the needs of the particular group, with a few unwavering elements. The focus is on assets—not what is missing but what we have—namely, what we do that is right and how each asset is linked to others that are right.

Steps of the Asset Mapping Process

Each teacher is given a map, with assets organized in three categories: school culture, faculty, and students (see Figure 6–1). Each teacher ranks where she sees the school for each item. Then teachers form small groups to discuss each item on the map and where they place themselves, the school, and the students along the continuum from 1 to 10. Conferring with colleagues, often from different grade levels, teachers adjust their responses to fall within a five-point spread to achieve a more workable set of data with clear patterns and concentrations.

ASSETS EVIDENT WHEN TEACHING AND LEARNING ARE ALIGNED WITH RESEARCH

	1 LOWEST ←	2	3	4	5	6	7	8	9	10 HIGHEST →
SCHOOL CULTURE PROMOTES:										
collaboration and shared leadership between all faculty members and the community										
faculty and students working together to create a school-wide environment that reflects values about teaching and shared learning										
an atmosphere of rigor, inquiry, and intimacy										
meaningful communication and interaction between the school, parents and the community										
flexibility in structures in order to accommodate learners' needs, including teachers' needs for professional development										
regular, intellectually interesting discourse including discussion about student work										
awareness of colleagues' assets										
faculty members who view themselves as learners, demonstrate these characteristics										
faculty concurs about content standards										

Figure 6–1: *Asset Map*

ASSETS EVIDENT WHEN TEACHING AND LEARNING ARE ALIGNED WITH RESEARCH

	1 LOWEST ←	2	3	4	5	6	7	8	9	10 HIGHEST →
FACULTY:										
focus instruction on a few concepts over a long period of time										
create opportunities for students to learn and apply concepts in contexts other than the classroom										
create classroom and library environments that reflect student learning and are conducive to student engagement										
organize learning materials so they are readily accessible to students										
use a wide variety of descriptive assessment tools including observation										
model the thinking processes used by proficient learners—think aloud, share their own learning experiences										
expect the highest quality work from students, maintain rigorous performance standards										
understand instructional strategies and assessment necessary to meet state/district content standards										
create opportunities to meet with students individually, in small, and in large groups										

Figure 6–1: *Asset Map (continued)*

109

ASSETS EVIDENT WHEN TEACHING AND LEARNING ARE ALIGNED WITH RESEARCH

	1 LOWEST ←—	2	3	4	5	6	7	8	9	10 HIGHEST —→
STUDENTS:										
retain and reapply major concepts and thinking strategies after instruction										
describe their thinking processes and know how being metacognitive helps them learn										
describe areas of passionate interest and seek to learn more										
work intently for long periods of time										
have opportunities to apply/share learning in a variety of ways										
engage in problem solving and assume responsibility for solving learning problems										
create mental images to help them understand concepts										
ask relevant, penetrating questions										
synthesize during and after the learning of a new concept										
distinguish important from less important concepts										

Figure 6–1: *Asset Map (continued)*

ASSETS EVIDENT WHEN TEACHING AND LEARNING ARE ALIGNED WITH RESEARCH

	1 LOWEST ←	2	3	4	5	6	7	8	9	10 HIGHEST →
STUDENTS:										
use a variety of techniques to infer and defend inferences										
make connections between the new and the known										
describe high standards/ways they are meeting the standards										
are aware of content standards towards which their daily work is oriented										

Copyright © 2002 PEBC

Figure 6–1: *Asset Map (continued)*

If the long lists of assets prove too cumbersome and long, teachers can condense items or spread discussions over several meetings. The map is more a guide to process and structure than prescribed content, although the assets, derived from research of successful schools, usually turn out to be most useful. The key is that discussion occurs around what leads to success, how different assets are linked to each other, and a consensus about rankings and goals for the school.

Discussion may be the most crucial part of this process. It is in conversation that teachers see how their colleagues view the school and begin to identify connections and links between what they see for students, for teachers, and for the school culture. They can get to the deeper questions, to the reasoning and rationale behind their rankings and connections.

Once the data sets are completed, each small group places sticky dots on a wall-sized copy of the asset map to indicate where their group determined their ranking according to each category and item. Then the whole group gathers to look at frequency distribution and consider the following questions for discussion:

- What do you notice?
- What, if any, connections exist between the three maps?
- Where is there agreement? Where is there disagreement?
- What assets are emerging as potential goals and why?
- How do the assets connect with and support standards?

Often, when the teachers gather in front of the wall-sized asset map to look at where the sticky dots appear, they notice that they place themselves in a higher range in instructional items, and rank student-related learning were much lower. The questions bubble up. Where was the connection between the teaching and the learning? If the teachers were generally following so many of the best practice ideals, why wasn't it showing in the students' learning? As a tool, the asset map reveals overlooked areas of thinking and observations.

The facilitator, who can be a staff developer, administrator, or teacher, encourages the exploratory nature of the discussion by:

- mirroring and paraphrasing what teachers are saying;
- identifying threads and contradictions as well as patterns;
- encouraging exploration of definitions and meanings; and
- supporting teachers who are grappling with frustration over ambiguous findings.

From the information provided by the rankings and discussion, the group identifies areas to improve and chooses two or three focal points for either the semester or the year. These then become the agreed-upon goals that they hope the professional learning will help them achieve. These goals are written in a wall-sized asset map format which is used as a structure to track and hold data from different sources.

Once a month during the upcoming year, time is set aside (optimally during faculty meetings) for each teacher to record and post anecdotes from observations and interactions that offer evidence of progress toward those two or three goals.

The evidence can come from diverse sources including:

- standardized test data
- district assessments with reading inventories and writing samples
- records of attendance at parent conferences, back to school nights, family literacy nights
- teachers' anecdotal records
- observations of teaching and learning
- notes from faculty meetings
- questions that arise

In this way, teachers are regularly reminded of what they are striving to achieve and thus establish a habit of watching for evidence of progress or regress. This is authentic, ongoing assessment. If they don't see progress one month, they can look at what was happening, refocus, and revise. Like mile markers on the highway, the anecdotal records help track movement throughout the year.

The wall-sized asset map is also a visual documentation for visitors, parents, funders, and others who might provide support for the school's efforts. The accumulation of data drawn from both qualitative and quantitative sources provides a powerful picture. Ideas are shared and successes celebrated through this collaboratively maintained record of work that has occurred and changes that have resulted.

A school community can track their progress using the asset map and following these basic principles and suggestions:

- Collect data of many kinds to support evaluation.
- Suggest a specific direction by keeping an eye on agreed-upon, explicit goals.
- Invite all members of the school community to participate so that all share responsibility. At the least, share and discuss with full faculty.
- Use a visual guide and measure of success.
- Repeat the process at the end of each year to provide both summative data for the current year and formative data to plan for the next year.

At the beginning of this chapter, I identified assessment possibilities that support best instructional practice. The asset-mapping process gives teachers

- a way to know students,
- a vehicle for combining information from different types of data collection,
- a plan that is guided and implemented by the people who are affected by it,
- a method to use data on an ongoing basis to inform instruction,
- a system to look simultaneously at data on teacher and student change, and
- a visual document that clearly communicates findings.

The evidence of instructional efficacy leading to student learning eliminates the possibility of a void to be addressed by outside agencies. Instead, reasonably accurate assessment of current practice guides professional learning and practice.

Sustaining Effective Practice

Sound assessment is key to sustaining a commitment and especially urgent today, when changes in administration, funding sources for professional development, increased directives from the district, and strictures on federal funding mean continual pressure to change in direction, program, and focus. With valid data providing evidence of instructional practice that positively impacts student learning, a course can be laid that fits the context of the individual school. Two questions we continually hear are What do we hold on to? What needs to change? Finding ways to integrate the new into the old may appear to drain time and energy but, in the end, will save more time and energy than was initially required.

Once schools have made decisions about continued direction based on credible assessment data, structures helpful in maintaining the momentum of new learning and practice can be organized in three ways:

1. Share with others in and outside your building to foster continued clarity and reflection on practice and purpose.
   - In-house labs, described earlier in the book, provide an opportunity to work as a faculty on instructional expertise.
   - Hosting visitors from other schools. Mary Acosta says, "When visitors are here, I'm really aware of each thing I do and say . . . I think of them sitting there watching and I think: What are they seeing?"
   - Inviting teachers from neighboring schools to join a study group builds a wider network of collaboration and professional ideas.

2. Continue the conversation with a focus and awareness on goals. As long as professional dialogue about instruction continues, so does the potential for learning and growth.
   - Inservices at crucial times such as before school starts or shortly thereafter and at the end of the year provide an opportunity to establish whole school goals and the steps to reach those goals in the upcoming year.
   - Faculty meetings can be consistently dedicated and structured to focus on professional learning.
   - Grade-level and cross-grade-level team meetings allow for specific, age-appropriate curriculum planning as well as looking at developmental curriculum planning.
   - Study groups and Critical Friends Groups provide both collaborative and professional learning through ongoing focused questioning, reflection, and feedback around instruction, student work, and professional reading.

3. Take on new roles and relationships with professional development organizations and individuals. Continued professional relationships with colleagues outside of the building prevent insularity and sustain the energy and pace of a focused continual learning and improvement process.
   - Short-term consultants may have some use, but Judith Warren Little urges forming sustained partnerships as an important component of school-based professional development. Networks provide courage as well as knowledge.
   - When professional development is seen as more than training, ways to continue to grow and learn are seen as essential to a professional life, "from staff development as a 'frill' that can be cut during difficult financial times to staff development as an essential and

indispensable process without which schools cannot hope to prepare young people for citizenship and productive employment" (Sparks 1994).

- Teachers who have worked with a professional development model are often asked to become staff developers for other teachers. Cooperative administrators make arrangements for teachers to get limited time off from their classrooms to work in another school. As staff developers, they continue to be part of the dialogue and exploration into effective instructional practice and can bring that dialogue back to their colleagues. They also hone their skills, clarify their thinking, and deepen their understandings, which they can also share with colleagues.

As complex as the change process may seem, holding on to what has worked while pressures for new programs continue to appear requires that teachers have time to revisit their beliefs and goals for teaching and learning. These beliefs and goals provide a basic constancy from which develops an overarching instinct for marrying old strengths with fresh ideas. New innovations are always being discovered; thinking outside of, but not necessarily discarding, old boxes is always a good idea. In the end, and perhaps hardest of all, educators in the field sometimes take a stand and hold their ground for what they see and believe is ultimately in the best interests of the children.

Chapter 7

The Voices of Foster Elementary School

Stories ground complicated ideas in concrete terms, they give them a flesh and blood reality.

—Terrence Deal and Kent Peterson, *The Leadership Paradox*

Guiding Questions

What communitywide systems and agreements are in place or being considered?

What consistency and inconsistency do you see throughout the school in relation to an instructional model, approach, and philosophy?

What is your own willingness or interest with regard to new instructional practice?

What leadership does your school provide to support logistics for professional learning and experimentation and to push the boundaries of thinking and learning?

What would you say are your goals for student learning?

How could you assess progress toward those goals?

What will you never give up?

The story of one school community's transformation, steps they took, and how they responded to what they encountered along the way, provides signposts to help others move more quickly on their own path. At Foster Elementary School in Arvada, Colorado, we see the potential for improvement when school community members make well-informed decisions about their own course for professional learning and growth.

These are the threads of the stories the teachers weave about their years spent studying their art and craft. The stories do not answer every question or solve every problem but they present a significant picture of self-sustaining and renewing effort that encourages hope for the possibilities.

We see the power of school community members charting a course that encompassed:

- A focus on instruction as the foundation and driving force of all that occurs
- Explicit communitywide understanding of the purpose for learning and the steps to take
- Leadership to support the plan
- Time to read, think, and talk with colleagues
- Discussion of the challenges, obstacles, and constraints that are part of the process
- Ongoing spark to continue learning

Foster Elementary School has served as a model for many other schools in the Denver area and across the country. The concrete steps and activities in which these adults engaged have been replicated successfully and effectively in other schools. They can be summarized by the following principles:

- Meaningful, effective instruction is the essential building block for a flourishing school.
- Working partnerships between individuals build strong connections in the whole school.
- Credibility is established through an articulated and demonstrated effective instructional model.
- Leadership distributed among school community members makes it possible to sustain commitment.
- Thinking and learning increase with consistency and continuity throughout the school.
- Fun is essential.

Foster Elementary:
Historical Context and Background

The history of Foster Elementary School is a common one. Erected in 1955 to serve a developing neighborhood of middle- and working-class households, Foster looks like many other schools built in the first decades after World War II—a plain, one-story, brick Y-shaped building with a parking lot in front.

The original Foster families and teachers all spoke the same language (English) and shared the same cultural values and background, but beginning in the late 1970s, the population of the neighborhood began to change and continued to change again and again. Groups of immigrants replaced the original homeowners, and children arrived with a multitude of language and cultural backgrounds that were unfamiliar to the teachers. Many of these children were not prepared to adjust to the demands of the mainstream American school environment.

Carla Stolzfuz, a teacher at Foster since 1982, recalls that with the change in students' backgrounds, "I questioned my capacities as a teacher." As a result of the changes, some teachers hung on, but many came and went quickly. Principals didn't last long either; Foster became the last stop before retirement or the first stop before moving to a school with more potential for "success."

In those days, the doors to the classrooms were closed, which meant no natural light touched the wide hallways. I have heard some people refer to memories of feeling unsafe. There was no focused conversation about instruction or discipline, nor was there schoolwide consistency for students as they moved from class to class and grade to grade.

A Visit to Foster Today

These days, Foster's residential neighborhood is contained on one side by Wadsworth Boulevard, an eight-lane corridor lined with big box stores that runs for seemingly endless miles north to south. The neighborhood surrounding the school consists of blocks of small houses; two trailer parks that serve as entryways for recent immigrants; two apartment complexes, including subsidized housing; and a fertilizer plant.

Inside the school building, a feeling in the air of life, vitality, and enthusiasm greets the visitor. The feeling is so immediate and strong that a visiting teacher from a more affluent school exclaimed to her principal, "I want our building to feel like this!" The hallways are still wide and windowless but now sunlight from the classroom windows spills through open doorways to light up the inner hallways. Students' work—writing and visual art—lines the walls. There are always adults and children moving through the hallways, pausing to chat or notice something together. People smile with pleasure at each other when they pass.

As you walk by classrooms, you hear a variety of voices and the hum of students talking about their thinking, asking questions, and offering suggestions with diverse accents and languages. You see a variety of skin shades and different ethnic features. You hear laughter. You see students gathered on the floor, leaning over each other's desks as they work together or observe how a classmate is accomplishing a task.

You might see Tom Figliolino, the head custodian, helping a child with a project that requires specialized tools. If you stop to look at the work on the walls, you are likely to be joined by a child who will explain how and why they created those pieces. When Jerry Knox, the nighttime custodian, arrives, he marks the end of the school day for teachers with his conversational checking in about how the day has gone. In the cafeteria, you see posters related to reading comprehension strategies with words describing sensory images of the food served for lunch. Everyone in the building is part of the teaching effort.

Looking out the music-room window around to the back of the building, between the school and the community center where parents come for classes and children meet for after-school activities, is a large patch of worked soil that, depending on the time of year, sustains carefully tended plants at varying stages of growth. A new outdoor amphitheater for student and community performances is located next to a miniature wildlife habitat. Picnic tables sit under trees alongside chess tables built by a parent who ran the after-school chess club. Parents come and go to tend the garden, teach, or take classes at the community center. There is an evolving and ongoing effort to create an increasingly welcoming environment for children and their families as well as visitors from other schools and the community.

Foundation for Growth

In 1990, Pauline Bustamante arrived at Foster with a dream to build a strong school community. Her leadership attracted new teachers who wanted to work at Foster precisely because of the needs and challenges. Teachers like Marcia Hecox "knew that something big could happen." When students have greater needs to be met or challenges to overcome in their schooling, teachers must draw more heavily on their own capacities to meet the challenge. For some educators, Pauline's dream and determination to create a strong and vibrant community offered a compelling reason to work at Foster.

Pauline began slowly with specific steps to establish a cohesive community. She led the way to create a community center for families. Starting as a group of neighbors who wanted a place to get together, talk, and drink coffee, the center evolved into a setting for agency providers of human resources, ESL classes, and a place for parents to take GED classes while their children were in preschool. Eventually, this building became the site for adult English language classes, the arts, and athletic activities outside of the school day for about 750 students from three area schools.

In school, Pauline established consistent disciplinary procedures and rules with clear boundaries and consequences. Children could rely on being safe everywhere in the school.

Pauline established a committee structure to ensure that teachers shared genuine responsibility for the direction and growth of the school community through a consensual decision-making process and distributed leadership structures. With Pauline, they gained dignity in their work and enjoyed her respect for their abilities. She also helped teachers realize their own dreams. When Marcia came to Foster as a Title One math teacher, she suggested an inclusion model where Title One teachers worked in the classroom in partnership with the classroom teacher rather than pulling students out for special services. Pauline gave her both moral and logistical support to try it. Marcia recalls that it was a big step to change to partner teaching. She started with two teachers, and once they saw it was a good way to get help for their students, other Title One teachers approached classroom teachers and were eventually welcomed in every classroom. The reward of providing a better experience for the children made the effort worthwhile to everyone.

Each of these changes—true inclusion of families, schoolwide consistency, distributed leadership, and in-classroom collaboration—provided the seeds for further school improvement.

Recognizing and Implementing the Next Step: Focus on Instruction

With the achievement of a strong community, coinciding with a directive from the district to submit a schoolwide improvement plan, Pauline asked Mary Ross and Marcia Hecox to attend a meeting to learn about PEBC as an option for staff development. Mary and Marcia liked the description of in-school staff development they heard at this meeting and decided to present the idea to their colleagues.

123

Marcia remembers, "That was the most horrifying meeting because we proposed this huge change for people. And (to our relief) most people went along with it, and the people who didn't agreed not to block. . . . We followed a collaborative decision-making process." Then Pauline announced her retirement.

"When Pauline left," Marcia recalls, "Mary and I thought, 'All of this is going to stop. What are we going to do?' Pauline said to us one time, 'You need the next step.' Our new principal, Joy Hood, did take us to the next step."

Joy brought organized methods for teachers to look at student achievement. With clear beliefs about best instructional practice based in research and experience, Joy provided the leadership to systematically identify what was and wasn't working toward that achievement with new ways to support continual improvement and innovation. She asked teachers to choose one focus within which everything else would fit and then to take the next step toward instructional efficacy.

A Homegrown Initiative for Schoolwide Improvement

With a twenty-day contract for a PEBC staff developer to be in their school, the Foster faculty took their next step toward increased instructional efficacy. Stephanie Harvey and Ellin Keene provided regularly scheduled in-classroom demonstration lessons centered on reading and incorporating writing.

The teachers at Foster recall that from the very beginning, Stephanie's enthusiasm and clarity about steps for leading students in building both content and process knowledge motivated them as their expectations and beliefs about possibilities for their teaching and their students' learning began to shift.

Around the middle of that first year, they received a directive to choose a model for Comprehensive School Reform Design. After a committee attended a showcase of potential programs, they came up with an idea to extend the work with

PEBC to a whole school reform model. Rather than start over with a completely new program, they could build on what they had already begun. Ellin Keene told them that while nobody had researched the comprehension strategies in any area but reading, she knew a teacher who was teaching one strategy through every curricular area and he was finding that his students were making more connections to their learning and retaining more of what he had taught. Ellin suggested it was a good time to begin experimenting with a new kind of integration around thinking strategies. The teachers were excited about the potential for common language across disciplines, grade levels, and classrooms. From their positive experience with a schoolwide discipline model, they knew that repetition and consistency were powerful tools for student learning.

They embarked on a series of planning meetings that involved different groups over a period of a few months. They began by identifying their current state, then talked about their desired state and how they would achieve that. Teachers continued to pose questions and refine a plan for a whole school design.

Meanwhile, demonstration lessons and ongoing staff development continued. Stephanie and Ellin offered lessons with specific strategies and skills. In this way, teachers got actual experience in learning more about the model while looking at how to develop a comprehensive, long-term plan.

Comments recorded by Mary Ross at an early meeting reflect an openness and a readiness to embark on a new pathway and partnership. They identified systems, attitudes, an instructional model, a time frame, and an assessment plan. By March, they identified three specific areas for focusing their planning:

- Financial support: grant with the Rose Foundation
- Assessment: include asset mapping
- Goal: develop Foster as a lab school

Joy continued to lead the faculty in conversations to develop and articulate their beliefs about teaching and learning in order to guide them through the creation of their "homegrown" Comprehensive School Reform Design plan. From these conversations, they created a document articulating their firm beliefs, which became the touchstone for all future decision making.

At a staff meeting in March, the question was asked, "Why are we excited about PEBC?" Articulating their motivation was key because it was going to be up to them to make this thing happen, make it work, and keep it going. The comments addressed the accessibility of the new ideas for teacher understanding and implementation:

- "Strategies are accessible."
- "Excellent demonstrations—I even write down the words she says."
- "Answers to little procedures. I implement these and my classroom is changed."
- "Appreciate seeing this because of my lack of experience."
- "The direction of the school district and PEBC meshes."

and the most significant, immediate impact on students.

- "A child of mine [for whom] writing is difficult, but on the state assessment she wrote, 'glittering light on the ocean.'"
- "When I look at the faces of my children, I see the delight in their eyes."
- "Children question more and predict, using the terminology."
- "This pulls in the difficult students."
- "Students are applying new learning on their own."

Finally, teachers spoke about the impact on the school community and mentioned sharing and consistency.

- "I see the whole school. Students can talk more deeply and have more to say. Students look happy, more relaxed."
- "As teachers, we are sharing more of our hearts. Consequently, students are sharing more, too."

Mary's notes continue to reflect the wide net of collaboration cast in the development of this project. If the faculty had chosen one of the federally approved CSRD programs, they could have applied for federal funds to support it rather than seeking private funding. But that didn't stop them from creating what they thought would be most effective for their school. District administrators joined the planning meetings to provide ideas and support for coordinating this directive with district directives. With PEBC's help, they sought funding from local sources. Eventually, the Rose Community Foundation agreed to support this as a pilot program.

Ellin recalls: "We knew this was going to be different than what we had done before—not just one teacher at a time—this was going to be everyone." Joy remembers it was a "whole staff effort all the time."

A Powerful Beginning: The Summer Institute

This was the beginning of truly being interested in everyone's thinking.

—Mary Acosta

A leadership team composed of Joy, staff developers, and teachers developed an implementation plan based on identified needs, resources, and the whole faculty's decision to focus on one comprehension strategy at a time. They had read *Nonfiction Matters* (Harvey 1998) and realized that questioning and wondering were key to deepening thinking and understanding. With a grant from Oracle to purchase ninety computers with Internet access, they were poised to engage in the research process at all grade levels. The leadership team knew they wanted a powerful and inspiring launch of the new initiative and the new year.

From *Nonfiction Matters*, they had become intrigued with the idea of passion as it derives from and leads to authentic curiosity and discovery. They decided to begin the year with an exploration of personal passions. Joy sent an invitation to everyone who worked in the building with a request that they attend the Summer Institute for which she would provide a stipend to compensate them for their time. She asked that they think about their passions in preparation for their participation.

Day One: What Is Your Passion?

The first morning, Joy facilitated a discussion in which people described their areas of passion. She remembers people "talking from their hearts." For people who had worked together for years and for those who were new to the school, this discussion led them to new ways of knowing each other.

In the afternoon, everyone researched and engaged in one of their identified passions. They also watched and took notes on their own process of exploration—where and how they struggled and succeeded—in order to identify potential roadblocks as well as steps to success that might better help students succeed in their own research projects in the fall.

With music teacher Molly Niven's suggestion that there be a visible representation of each person's passion, everyone created an interactive set of artifacts that reflected questions, interest, and expertise. These were displayed in the hallways at the beginning of the school year. For Caryl Hawkins, "beginning with passions and having all our posters up in the hall was an immediate community-building activity."

Each classroom teacher began the year with students discussing passions and developing visible representations. Students began to see interests they shared with their teachers and everyone began to talk about passions. "Then," Caryl says, "we were experts and we helped each other with pursuits of study and activities."

Day Two: Instructional Content

Ellin brought a complex and difficult article that would challenge teachers' understanding. During the time allotted for them to read the article, some of them got up to sharpen their pencils or even went out in the hall to talk. Very few really tackled it. Ellin recalls having to make a decision to set the tone for the degree of rigor in her work with the teachers at Foster. She took a calculated risk and pointed out that they were avoiding the struggle with a difficult text and suggested that this struggle is what they ask of students every day. The teachers realized firsthand the amount of hard work, effort, and risk taking involved in pushing beyond their current capacity. When they settled down to work with the challenging text, they began to identify strategies and skills that they could share to help students work through challenges. They also began to see themselves as hard-working scholars with deep intellectual capacity.

Day Three: Planning and Assessment

Goals for the year ahead were drawn from asset map discussions around perceived strengths and gaps in the school culture and around teacher practice to support student learning. They decided which elements in the three categories were most important to them for the year ahead.

Students: retain and reapply major concepts and thinking strategies after instruction; can describe their own thinking processes and know how being metacognitive helps them learn; synthesize as they are learning and after they have learned a new concept; can describe areas of passionate interest and seek to learn more in these areas; ask relevant, penetrating questions.

Faculty: focus on a few concepts of great consequence over a long period of time; model the thinking processes used by proficient learners—think aloud, share their own learning experiences; use and analyze a wide variety of descriptive assessment tools including observations.

School culture: promotes awareness of colleagues' assets; promotes meaningful communication and interaction between the school, parents, and community; promotes collaboration and shared leadership between all faculty members and the community; promotes an atmosphere of rigor, inquiry, and intimacy.

The asset map was further extended and developed through Joy's ideas and staff implementation until it became a way to focus conversation and regularly maintain a chronological accumulation of different kinds of data throughout the year. The teachers set their sights on the elements identified and agreed upon at this meeting.

The three days of the Summer Institute built a community of people with a shared sense of purpose and understanding gleaned from learning more about themselves and each other. Perhaps most dramatically, the Institute set a precedent for rigorous intellectual inquiry and discussion. The teachers were ready to take their first steps on the path toward clear, specific goals and a shared vision ahead.

Learning from Many Sources

> You can't help people grow if you don't think they can, because you are going to find ways to help prevent them from growing. Encourage people to push limits, to try to take that step because that's when they are really free. Now if you're free you aren't afraid to learn from everybody and anybody. (Horton 1998)

Staff Development Team

During the first year of the whole school reform, Ellin Keene and Cheryl Zimmerman were the primary staff developers with support for technology from Jonathan Bender and in close collaboration with Joy and the leadership team. Each person brought unique qualities and strengths to bear in their influence with the teachers and school.

Ellin is passionate and animated; teachers forget they are worn out or discouraged when she is in the room with them.

Ellin's energy is like wet, sticky snow that calls you to make forts and snowmen and angels. She bestows her joy and appreciation on everyone in the room, making students and adults feel they are brilliant, worthy, fascinating. Ellin makes the job of teaching and learning seem exciting every moment. She still argues fervently and falls in love with each class of students and their thinking.

Cheryl is just as passionate but with a steadier burn and quiet determination, more like dry snow that is beautiful and awe-inspiring and that draws you to contemplate and revel in the pleasure of the world. Her strength is still and evolutionary. Cheryl's patience and willingness to carefully listen leads everyone to talk until they find clear directions. She gathers all the thoughts and then provides clear, succinct guidance. She really understands children's strengths, and it is in her work with them that you see the fervor and expertise. You know when you work with Cheryl that she is positively there to do what is best for the school and the students.

Cheryl recalls, "We developed personal relationships over time. We knew about each other's lives outside of school and made connecting in that way a priority." The staff developers became members of the community with the result that their work with the teachers was not seen as an extra occasional piece but as a seamless thread in the teachers' ongoing practice and progress. As the teachers had hoped for in an earlier meeting, there was a strong PEBC presence in the school.

Contours of Leadership

Countless avenues for assuming a leadership role remained open to every person in the building. Throughout the years, different people have assumed leadership roles for different purposes—from providing the spark for rigorous or divergent thinking in a discussion, to conscientiously holding to norms for how to talk about students, to coming up with a startling solution to a thorny problem, to being the first to try something new in the classroom or in their own learning. Just as

Linda Lambert suggests, "If leadership is everyone's work, it does not require extraordinary charismatic qualities and uses of authority" (1998a).

Teacher-Leaders

Even with so many natural leaders in the building, there was a still a need for more formalized leadership structures. In years one and two, teachers volunteered to serve on the Leadership Committee that included teachers to represent grade levels and curricular areas, Joy, and the PEBC staff developers. Their role was representative, so with input from colleagues, they identified and planned for points of focus and direction.

In the third year, with Joy's retirement and the transition to new principal Carolyn Abey, Mary Ross agreed to serve as a designated liaison between the school and PEBC staff development team. She was the contact person for problem solving and any other details of staying on track with the big-picture vision. Mary's tall willowy frame, gentle smile, and diplomatic manner belie a strong and unyielding inner resolve about what is right for students and how to help the teachers do what they need to be doing. She is an unwavering advocate for the community and an inveterate grant writer. Mary arranged schedules and consulted with staff developers about progress and plans along the way. She brought a particular dedication and sincerity to sustaining and connecting professional learning and change in practice.

The following year, strong work routines and relationships were well established with teachers and staff developers and the responsibility could be distributed more widely. Title one partner-teachers who worked with several teachers served as liaisons to talk with staff developers and help plan for the days they would come to Foster. Displaying flexibility and adapting to the current realities, leadership roles and, hence, power and influence, changed each year with shifting needs and resources.

Administrative Leadership

The stories and descriptions of Joy Hood's work during her first two years offer a model for many aspects of effective instructional leadership. Joy combined care and understanding for everyone with knowledge of research and solid experience in the classroom. Like Mary Ross, Joy holds an unyielding commitment to a critical level of instructional efficacy and a determination that teaching meet every child's need. She served the teachers by attending to the big picture as well as the details of their goals at every step along the way. She created a learning environment for adults as well as for children. And, not least important, Joy infused her ideas and actions in the school with a sense of humor and fun.

Mary Ross says that Joy was instrumental in the school's success because she always brought the content of the work with PEBC to every staff meeting, "allowing for good conversations that led people to think more and more deeply. She was relentless." Joy realized that "We had to have this in our lives, not just in our heads." She modeled an intellectual curiosity and liveliness, attending all study groups, using cognitive strategies throughout the school and in her own work. Joy also brought thought-provoking books and excerpts from books she was reading to faculty meetings and continued Pauline's tradition of reading aloud at these meetings.

Everyone seems to agree that Joy's most crucial contribution was asking the hard questions that prompted deep and ongoing learning. This helped Susan McIver, a primary Title One teacher, see what she needed to do for her students. She realized that "if you don't ask the hard questions, you're not going to get deep." And if you don't go deep, learning remains on the surface and can slide away pretty easily.

Having "gone deep," they didn't want to let their learning go, and when Joy retired after the first two years, many wondered what would happen in the transition to a new principal who was not experienced with the instructional model. The reality is that while learning relies on the people involved, structures and commitments have to become so ingrained in a school culture, even in the school building, that they have a life of their own beyond a particular individual's ability to sustain them for the group. After her second year, new principal Carolyn Abey reflected on the state of the initiative: "It looks like it's not just principal driven now but it's staff driven and what I hope to be able to do is keep everything flowing."

A Continuum of Participation

> Teachers were either open to learning "right now" or open to saying they would hang back for awhile until they were certain it wasn't just another fad in the field.
>
> —Cheryl Zimmerman

Teachers from Foster repeatedly stress their appreciation at being allowed to set their own pace for implementing change while continuing to think and talk about it. Carla mentions, "it wasn't like someone saying: 'Tomorrow you're going to do it.'" That is, of course, unless they wanted to leap into change in their classrooms. Then, they received support in the form of labs, school visits, demonstration lessons, inservice days, and rigorous conversation to help them learn and sustain the effort.

Several teachers took the first leap. They volunteered their classrooms for demonstration lessons; started trying to incorporate the comprehension strategies into their instruction; participated in every opportunity to read, talk, and observe. They were able to tolerate a level of discomfort, dissonance, and confusion in their professional lives. They could stand to be temporarily knocked off balance as they stepped into realms they didn't yet fully understand.

Ellin's memories of Molly Niven's leadership role offer a picture of the potential influence of one teacher on the whole community. The explicit instructional model gave Molly, who taught music and physical education, a welcome opportunity to connect with the classroom teacher's work. She quickly grasped how to use the reading comprehension strategies as thinking strategies to support her instruction. As a collaborative professional, she knew that if she used the same language, she could support the students' learning in their classrooms. The comprehension strategies are prominently posted on her music room walls along with the elements of music. Whether teaching volleyball or elements of music, Molly uses thinking strategies to support understanding and learning. Moreover, Molly contributed ideas for classroom teachers to offer nonverbal forms of processing and expression to deepen comprehension in literacy.

Since Molly worked with all the students, it made sense to her to organize whole school events such as assemblies where students created presentations around a strategy they used for reading or writing, which were subsequently displayed on posters in the hallways, so that the messages continued to impact the community.

Molly also pushed for an expanded vision of teaching and learning in study groups and among the leadership team by bringing in articles on new research about the brain and kinesthetic learning.

At another end of the continuum, Mary Acosta, a solid teacher with many years' experience, serves as the poster child for early resistance. She tells visiting principals, "I was your worst nightmare. I really wanted to just see what it was going to be about . . . I thought, 'Oh yeah, everybody's supposed to be gung ho about this and then so what? Next year it won't be here anyway and we'll go back to our own thing again.'" Joy told her to at least participate in the discussions with an open mind.

Andrea Holten, Mary's partner-teacher, watched demonstration lessons and brought ideas back into the classroom. Then Mary began to notice changes in the way students were thinking and how they were able to hold on to ideas. Andrea says, "Mary started going to demo lessons so we could talk more. We had a lot of lunch conversations." Mary's pathway to change was through learning from her colleague in the course of their work together.

Ellin remembers, "Mary started to share things that had happened in her classroom and almost in an 'Is this right? Is this it?' kind of way. She started coming to more meetings and study groups and asset-mapping meetings with stories about her students."

Each person in the school has her own story of her first big breakthrough in understanding the value and possibility for her students of professional development. It was a matter of believing, with conviction, that this was a worthwhile change for the better and of being given the opportunities to learn and be comfortable with the process before being forced to comply. Those who were "gung ho" were certainly at least mildly frustrated with those who were hanging back, but as long as no one set out to undermine the efforts of the leapers and no one showed disdain toward the watchers, they could work together within already established structures. Letting people decide where they would start on a continuum of involvement allowed them to control their learning and their teaching. Whichever perception of the new learning people had, they had to respect their colleagues' different perceptions.

For each person, growth was supported through time and training sufficient to find a comfort level within each opportunity to take the next leap and, eventually, everyone did.

A Framework for Professional Learning

With a commitment to growth and an increasing understanding of the particular instructional approach, teachers and students learned within a parallel framework grounded in elements of gradual release of responsibility and cognitive strategies.

Modeling

I'm cracking open my head so you can know what I'm thinking.

—Teacher's comment recorded on asset map for September

Demonstration Lessons

> When we began to have demonstration lessons, students started to share their thinking . . . huge light bulbs would go off for students we hadn't realized were capable of that thinking. They can all do it. I haven't come across anyone who can't.
>
> —Mary Young

Through demonstration lessons, teachers learned new methods and strategies for teaching, yet what they talk about first is a new view of who their students were and what they could do. Cheryl says, "With each demonstration, teachers increased the belief that their kids were indeed capable of deep thought." The combination of change in belief and expectation assisted by practical knowledge of how to support students' growth was key to inspiring change in teaching and learning.

Labs and School Visits

> We've gone to schools where we've seen really excellent teachers and we've all realized that there's more to learn.
>
> —Carla Stolzfuz

In any conversation with the teachers, I notice that they inevitably refer to another teacher they have visited or seen in a lab and how their teaching was influenced. Rather than reinventing the wheel over and over, these teachers have taken what others developed and refined and redefined it to fit their own style and students. Evidence of what the teachers have learned in other classrooms is prominent in the environment and tone as well as systems and structures. When they began welcoming visitors to their classrooms, it was clear that they not only learned an instructional model to use with their children but also absorbed ways of graciously and generously helping colleagues learn to be better teachers.

Practice: Learning from Experience

Teachers were learning from a variety of sources—from their own experiences as learners, as readers, and as writers; and from studies and research in particular issues of best practice. Cheryl remembers, "teachers began to stretch themselves as learners. [We] made many efforts to invite and involve them in learning as adults . . . some of the work rekindled passions, [the] desire to read and write, etc."

Cognitive Dissonance

> We struggled because there is a discomfort in figuring it out for yourself . . . it's not scary; it's okay that I don't know and okay to figure stuff out with the students.
>
> —Susan McIver

By using the strategies for their own reading and learning and allowing themselves to enter the discomfort zone of "not knowing," teachers came to a new relationship with their students' struggles—it's part of learning, exciting if you have the right support. Through using comprehension strategies for their own reading, they understood that the strategies were not newly invented concepts drawn from someone's imagination, but useful tools developed from studies of naturally proficient readers. Mary Young says, "It was such an eye opener. Oh, I do that when I read but I hadn't thought to share it with students."

Teachers began to discover authentic ways to use this approach to become proficient in any area of learning—particularly in areas that were challenging. They watched and questioned proficient learners in any endeavor or subject area to identify the strategies that could be articulated for others to use as well.

Guided Practice

Over the years, the concept of demonstration lessons expanded to include co-teaching in addition to observing. While staff developers continued to take the ultimate responsibility for planning and leading demonstration lessons, the teachers' participation during and in between lessons increased. Time and support for focused dialogue about these experiences continued to be crucial.

Thoughtful Reflection on Practice

Talking to each other—sharing, reflecting, questioning, and pushing their thinking—became an embedded and cherished part of the teachers' daily professional lives. They established agreements and rituals through numerous opportunities for both formal and informal interactions focused on teaching and learning.

Planning Conversations

Staff developers spent a significant percentage of their time planning with teachers. Collaborative planning was an aspect of everything they did, from demonstration lessons to study groups to inservices to the plan for the whole year.

When I first joined the team at Foster in their second year of whole school design they had decided to focus on developing sensory imagery as a strategy for comprehension, particularly in reading. Principal Carolyn Abey arranged for roving subs to cover each classroom while I met in two-hour blocks to plan with grade-level teams and for one hour with the two teachers who taught art, music, and P.E. Two hours allowed time to explore, brainstorm, and then formulate concrete plans and logistics.

Each team meeting followed a sequence of exploration, brainstorming, and problem solving prior to formulating a concrete content-rich and practical plan. We began with a general discussion of classroom needs and strengths including student background knowledge on which to build new learning.

Questions were aired about the specific strategy such as how to launch the exploration, how to expand their own grasp of how imagery enhances reading comprehension, and how to sustain and deepen the students' application in their lives. Concerns and hopes provided the focus for creating specific steps.

At the end of the two hours, each team had developed a plan that included daily activities thoroughly grounded in a stated purpose, context, and time frame. They also listed and divided preparatory tasks in a way that eased the burden for individual teachers. Finally, they planned opportunities for their own learning, including those that would be provided by staff developers.

After the meetings with teachers, I debriefed with Carolyn Abey and Mary Ross to design logistical support for the teachers' plans and goals, including opportunities for teachers to reflect on their own use of the strategy in reading and discuss their experiences teaching and using the strategy with students.

Study Groups

Study groups were a crucial contributing factor in the burgeoning intellectual climate at Foster Elementary School. In the first year, two different groups were offered. In one, participants read *The Quality School*, by William Glasser, a model that Joy had adopted in her previous school and had brought to Foster. In the other group, people read *Mosaic of Thought* (Keene and Zimmerman 1997). About twelve to fourteen teachers participated in each of the study groups. At each meeting they discussed the content of the books and tied it to their own work and then back to the content again. Occasionally, Ellin would facilitate, but generally, members of the group shared the responsibility. In the second year, the teachers at Foster extended an invitation to the teachers at the middle school, where most of their students went after sixth grade, in an effort to establish professional collegial relationships.

In subsequent years, books and articles were suggested by different people, often according to current burning questions that came up in meetings. Groups have read *Teaching with the Brain in Mind* by Eric Jensen, *A Framework for Understanding Poverty* by Ruby Payne, and numerous articles.

Through all the years, teachers have held fast to regular study-group meetings. Mary Young says, "I'm afraid I'm going to lose this direction and enthusiasm if I don't keep myself motivated so I participate in study groups and go to demonstrations for teachers."

Critical Friends Groups

In the summer after their fourth, and last, year with PEBC staff developers, three teachers—Barb Rodriguez, the literacy coordinator; Marcia Hecox, an intermediate teacher; and Caryl Hawkins, a primary teacher—attended the Critical Friends Group coaches training, and with volunteers in the fall, they started using protocols to look at dilemmas and instructional issues. With these structures, they were able to sustain a rigorous dialogue focused on instruction and student work with everyone sharing the responsibility that they had once relied on Joy to carry, of "asking the hard questions" and leading the thinking beyond the comfort zone.

The next summer, Carolyn extended the commitment and participation when she attended the training for administrators and primary teacher Lillian Serougi attended the coaches training. With these structured conversations, everyone shares the responsibility of instructional leadership and ongoing professional growth of the community.

Informal Conversations

Sometimes when I walk into the teacher's lounge at Foster during lunchtime, I am reminded of a passage from *The Fortunate Pilgrim* by Mario Puzo (1964), a semi-autobiographical novella Puzo wrote before his famous *Godfather* series: "They drank coffee and chatted together with that deep familiarity a close family feels. . . . "

Sharing ongoing experiences as they explore their own learning and endless anecdotes about their students' joys and failures, these teachers enjoy that same quality of closeness—a brief, rejuvenating interlude of professional and personal connection and reflection in the middle of a teacher's hectic day.

From the outset, there was a conscious effort to influence the conversation in the teacher's lounge so that it was inspiring and informative rather than discouraging and repetitive. Instead of dwelling on sad stories of obstacles blocking students' learning, they offered encouraging anecdotes and quotes that offered examples and expressed ideas for overcoming challenges.

Together and with the students, the community members' stance is, "We all value each other's voices and minds. I want to hear what you have to say."

Sustaining Progress

Assessment of Progress: Results for Students

Expectations of what students can do is going off the chart.

—Mary Young

When Joy first came to Foster, standardized test scores were in the low thirties (the percentage of children scoring "proficient" or above in skills assessed). No one disaggregated the data or looked at what each student needed. Under pressure to improve the school's numbers on the state test (which did increase), Joy asked, "How can we teach all students? How can we prepare all students to improve test scores in ways that wouldn't impact teaching in a negative way?" She used her foundational belief in teaching every child as a yardstick for assessing each proposed instructional plan.

Throughout the year, Joy also gathered data from attendance at parent conferences, back-to-school night, family literacy nights, disciplinary incidents, quotes from children, anecdotes from teachers and other visitors such as district literacy specialists, test scores, and samples of student work. This data was recorded monthly on a wall-sized asset map posted in the teacher's lounge. From this collection of numerical and narrative data, a cumulative picture of the school's change and progress was tracked and made concrete and visible to everyone.

Anecdotal evidence came from many sources. What the children said powerfully conveyed the sense that the community of learners had grown, and it was often the students' questions and thinking that most profoundly affected teachers' learning and led them to their next questions and steps. As

Lorraine Gutierrez noted, "When you give up control and let the kids come forth with their own thinking, it changes everything. I'm learning everyday from these kids."

Mary Acosta is bilingual and has welcomed several Spanish-speaking children into her classroom during the years. Mary commented that the other students never say "a critical word" about second language learners' efforts to speak English and, in fact, one of the quickest learners in the class said, "I want to learn Spanish so I can understand them."

Barb McCallister remembers, "Susan and I wanted to make sure that everyone was heard in the group discussions. Now when a child says something, we stop and talk about it. We don't just share and then go on. We also want the kids learning to facilitate their own discussion. We talked with them about that and we agreed as a group that the person who had the last comment would keep the conversation going. Now they ask, 'Who would like to go next?' and 'Who would like to add to my thinking?'"

One factor to consider in assessing impact is how students have changed as learners or more specifically in this case, as readers. Mary Young posed this particular question to her fifth-grade students. One boy replied, "Well, at one time, I would have just read it and said, 'I read it,' and put it down. Now I read it and think about it. That's what going deeper is. Those lingering thoughts."

One day, I walked into a classroom as they were wrapping up a poetry unit. The class was engaged in identifying elements of poetry. As we entered, fourth grader Anthony Ryden said, "Poetry is like . . . it's like your emotions are all caged up and a poem lets them all break out!"

I will never forget a ten-year-old boy who first came to Foster a month before the end of the school year. He had already suffered many losses in his young life and he was identified as having a borderline IQ. The structure and language provided by his teacher allowed him to make inferences of themes and metaphors and connections between books as a valued, respected participant in class discussions. The view of learning and knowing—of intelligence—was expanded. Asking questions, wondering, indeed "not knowing," were seen as signs of good learners.

Teacher Sandy Selzer noticed evidence that the kids had really gotten it at the beginning of the year when they were still using the language of the strategies to talk about texts. They were not just parroting back what they thought the teacher wanted to hear but rather using language to convey what they wanted to express. Furthermore, she was encouraged to see students explaining thinking strategies to other kids as a way to help them make sense of their reading.

Observations by visitors from outside the school are often an enlightening source of information. When Joy brought one of many groups of principals from PEBC schools to visit Foster in the fourth year, she recorded their observations, which she forwarded to the teachers:

- "Things seemed to be 'slowed down' in classrooms so that kids and teachers could really think."
- "We heard the same words being used by teachers and kids throughout the school. Bulletin boards, artwork, and posters used the same language that was being used by teachers and students."
- "Teachers modeled their thinking in every classroom; one even modeled her facial expression when she was thinking."
- "They are all being asked to think in depth (at a higher level) and question."
- "I hear 'we' from everyone."

When Jan Seahorn from the district assessment office observed as part of her research of schools that had adopted whole school designs, she noted:

- Teaching is focused.
- Students are engaged.
- Variety of assessments are used.

- Instruction is connected to assessment.
- Students use strategies across the curriculum.

With a multitude of sources for assessment, the adults in the building could look back to the dreams and hopes they had articulated at the early planning meetings for their "home-grown initiative," and identify what they had been able to accomplish.

In the fourth year of their school reform effort, genuine appreciation and attention for individual differences had created safety and an expectation that everyone will express his thoughts, ask questions, read, collaborate, observe in other classrooms, host visitors, and continue to push the limits of her own thinking and practice. Everyone in the building is a teacher and a learner. Mary Young says, "Sometimes they [her students] forget that I'm not one of them and they ask, 'What did you get?'"

Sustaining Independent Practice

There is a desire for the "old days" when the energy and excitement of the new initiative were everywhere. Our time with PEBC was very unifying and we were very proud of our school, our work, and our learning.

—Mary Ross

Through experiences as learners and as teachers, the adults at Foster Elementary developed firmly held beliefs about best practice, which they have sometimes struggled to sustain through changes in personnel and educational trends.

Cheryl observed that "at least a core group remained year after year, and they began to spearhead the work, fighting for the priority status to remain in spite of new leadership and new pressures."

Amidst other programs that have come from the district and the continually increasing pressure to raise test scores, teachers at Foster keep looking at how to incorporate the best practices that address all the different needs. With the support of Barb Rodriguez, a full-time literacy coach, they have also looked closely at transference and integration possibilities from what they have learned these past years. When they were told to use a particular program to teach reading, they continually searched for a way to incorporate strategy instruction into the new structure. They have studied how to most effectively help their students do well on state tests and now teach test-taking practice the way they would teach writing—by articulating explicit steps and thinking processes and identifying strategies and skills that each person needs to solve problems and answer questions.

As they began their fourth year of the initiative, new funding allowed them to hire several new teachers. While there was clearly a great benefit to smaller class size, there was also a concern about how to bring new faculty into the well-established community of learners who had shared so many experiences and so much learning and change over the years. A meeting with Sandy Selzer and Susan McIver to orient new teachers in the beginning of the year was followed by ongoing collaboration, the partner-teacher model, and opportunities for participation in book studies provided embedded support structures for new staff. Marcia says she knew it was working out when, at a meeting with a representative from the Rose Foundation, "it was the new teachers who were particularly vocal and forthcoming with anecdotes about how their instruction had changed and the impact they were seeing on children's learning."

With Carolyn Abey's retirement, they were once again looking for a principal to lead them as a rigorous community of learners and teachers. The hiring committee questioned candidates for the position about their familiarity with and support for PEBC and, most important, about the instructional philosophy and practice that that implies. They were able to hire Leigh Hiester, who comes from a school that has worked with PEBC for many years. She is deeply committed to helping teachers continue and extend their journey.

Lingering Question and Thoughts

At the beginning of the last year of Foster Elementary's grant, a program director from a foundation asked the teachers, "What's next? How do you go to the next deeper place?" That question resonated for months as teachers pondered and discussed how to definitively and completely answer it. They still bring it up with each other and with students. Marcia thought, "Next year we'll say, 'Okay, so we've gone this far. Now what do we do with it?' I don't think it's ever stopping. You always find some other way to use the strategy." Many of the teachers explain that they can "only know as they go what 'deeper' is." So they can't predict with certainty what they will find next—only that they will keep going.

The teachers at Foster have delved to the bottom of their souls, looked hard at failures, faced impossibilities and barriers with determination. No one has escaped the difficulties. No one has missed success. They have a dedication and a belief that keep them engaged in continuous growth and in being, really being, with their students and their work. They have held onto their beliefs about the essential elements that sustain their commitment. They are the ones who want to continue, so they drive the effort to sustain the initiative. They seek a variety of sources for new learning. And finally, they support each other to learn, take risks, and continually try new ideas.

A visit with Foster Elementary School shows us a variety of people performing in a variety of roles, all with the goal of student learning through thinking and understanding—aides and paraprofessionals, custodians, lunchroom workers, administrators, parents, volunteers, local police, and firemen. And finally, to complete a grand circle, the children have become the very best teachers. With their willingness, everyone continues to explore the endlessly surprising capacity of human learning.

Chapter 8

Meeting an Outstanding Challenge

You have to be pretty strong to say this is what I want to do.
It's felt like we were pushing against a wind pushing at us . . .
and still we felt our own power. We are driven to teach kids
well.

—Sandy Selzer

I sit with five young teachers on the patio of a restaurant in a trendy section of Denver. Today was to have been the final day of professional development for the year—a celebration of the learning that had occurred in their classrooms and the beginning steps for the future. They had clearly articulated their beliefs about learning and instructional practice after reading research and watching demonstration lessons. They had developed a skill set of best instructional practices. They had used multiple assessments to document student learning and developed their plan for the next year. This group of teachers had shown no limits in their willingness to do whatever was required to address the diverse needs of students in their besieged school.

Now, they are struggling. They have been informed that because the students' scores on the state test did not show adequate increase, their school will be closed or reorganized, their principal will definitely be transferred and a prescriptive instructional program will most likely be put in place for the following year.

Their faces usually radiate optimism and determination but today, sitting on the harshly bright patio, they are clearly terrified for their students and for their jobs. The sharp divide between the excitement and hopefulness of the previous week's meeting, when we had created a concrete plan for continued improvement, and the abyss they see ahead is humbling. I look at them with foreboding.

They consider their options, speculate about transfers to other schools or even leaving the profession. I do not want these teachers to be lost to the children who need them nor do I believe they should sacrifice themselves to a lost cause. Instead of instructional strategies and goals for professional learning, in this meeting, they need to talk about power, influence, and politics.

In our zeal to improve instruction, to explore best practice in teaching and the possibilities for learning, we had forgotten that our efforts are part of a bigger picture. And now that bigger picture is looming over us.

Perhaps there once was a time when teaching meant a lone adult behind closed doors in a classroom. If it was once true, it is increasingly less so. Two factors are triggering this change. First, research into effective schools is providing growing evidence that collaboration among teachers is a key component of effective schools—the school culture is a major influence on the quality of education. With collaboration, everyone's ideas and expertise gather to create a richer, more grounded perspective on best practice in a school. Furthermore, consistent processes, skills, and routines provide continuity for students from class to class and grade to grade so that they can build on previous knowledge rather than continually start over.

A second, and perhaps more disquieting factor is the increasing role of government agencies and policymakers in determining assessment for accountability measures, acceptable programs for curriculum, and instruction and rules that profoundly affect funding for particular schools and philosophical positions.

With this reach into the daily routines of classroom practice, both from within and outside of the building, teachers can no longer rest solely on their capacity for effectively working with their students. Outside forces, whether invited and welcomed or enforced and resisted, will either support or undermine a teacher's or school community's instructional decisions.

This is a hard chapter to write because I'm writing about an issue I haven't resolved and one that will most likely be a never-ending challenge to address. Here's what I know so far. This is not only about what I do but about who I am—my own strength, skill, and capacity for perseverance. This is about how I take a stand and hold my ground in winds of change— in the face of other people's adamant stories and points of view.

In recent years, a story has developed and taken root in the consciousness of our society that says that schools are failing, teachers are ill prepared, administrators are not to be trusted, and everyone in the profession is unwilling to look at what is effective. In schools, many tell tales of too much work, over-whelming challenges, and debilitating mandates. Everyone talks about the money—either too much wasted or not enough to go around.

Another story needs to be told with a louder voice. This story is about teachers who are respected conveyers of knowl-edge with an unwavering shared sense of purpose and clear pedagogy. It is about teachers with the skill to provide effec-tive learning experiences for diverse learners. It is about teach-ers who consider themselves to be, first of all, learners. If we are clear about our body of knowledge and skills and can offer evidence of actual teachers' and children's progress and achievement and how we continue to expand them, we can tell this story effectively. Still, I think it will take heroes to advo-cate for this story.

In *The Hero with a Thousand Faces*, Joseph Campbell (1972) describes the classic hero's journey as it has been passed down from diverse cultures. At the beginning of the hero's journey, the kingdom is in trouble and, while everyone else stands around complaining, the hero decides to do something about it. This hero is not so much a savior as an individual who is willing to endure challenges and overcome obstacles because he has heard a call for a quest that is too important to ignore.

The call may be in the form of a specific message or it may come as thoughts about what to do. It may be from a "dark and loathly" character. Like the rest of us, the hero often tries to ignore the call, not wanting to take on the effort and risks. But the call won't go away, and the hero finally heeds it and embarks on the road to adventure, otherwise known as the road of trials.

At the beginning of the journey, the hero must go through an initiation in order to prepare for the hard road ahead. As Campbell writes, "It is folly to go unprepared." Usually at least one important ally appears, and tools and gifts are offered. There is an initial obstacle to overcome to prove that the hero is ready to go. Then the challenges begin and they continue getting harder. There is always a juncture where the hero thinks she has overcome the challenges and has an easy road to the end, but then the worst comes along and she is in the belly of the beast, the dark night of the soul. This is the real crux of the hero's journey because the myth of the hero is ultimately a story of one's own inner struggles as a human being; the challenges, dragons, and demons are symbolic of our struggles in life. When the hero passes through this last phase and faces the scariest demon of all, the enemy is often transformed into an ally. Then the hero is called to return and share what he's learned with his community—his end reward is the sense of community.

The story of the hero offers a larger perspective on the challenges that educators face. Sometimes the journey is referred to as the Hero's Adventure. Perhaps that is the first lesson from the hero's journey. Thinking of the challenge as chosen—a daring adventure.

Lessons from the Hero's Journey

Lesson Number 1: Heed the Call

For anyone who has embarked on a challenging road toward an important destination, and I would argue that this includes everyone in education, the myth of the hero's journey offers a lens through which to view efforts as steps in a journey toward a crucial destination.

Heed your call. Think about what really grabs your attention. What keeps you getting up and going to school again each day? One middle school science teacher remarked, "I was a bank teller and I noticed all these teachers and they liked to learn and I thought that is what I would want to do. I knew I wanted to be a teacher."

Take one step at a time and continue to stop and check progress. Focus on what you can actually see and then see what you *can* do. If we know where we're going and we take each step to get there with clear frameworks, understanding, knowledge, and skills, we are bound to make progress.

Identify your own area for growth as a leader, advocate, and hero. I know that my own current area for growth is in the realm of politics. I have been closely watching people who are astute in that realm. It is especially helpful to me to watch a person with whom I have developed a relationship, so that I can talk with her about the thinking that leads to the effective actions. It is as if I am watching a demonstration lesson: observe the behavior, hear the thinking, try a small step on my own, and return to talk about it with the person I first observed.

An activity for leadership training adapted from a sequence developed by Joy Hood, guides (individuals or a group) to identify those heroic characteristics to which they might choose to aspire:

- Think about a person you know whom you would call a hero.
- What specifically does this person do?
- What are the qualities of what this person does?
- What are the categories of these qualities?
- Create an asset map that lists those categories as items on which to rank yourself.

- Pick one or two of these categories on which to focus your attention.
- Return to the list of behaviors you first identified. Identify the behaviors that fit into the categories you chose for your focus.
- Consider which of these behaviors you could try to implement.

Susie Sykes, a building resource teacher, identified a colleague as her hero and this is what she wrote: "When working with adults, remember to:

- maintain a reflective stance;
- ask probing questions rather than give answers;
- collaborate; and
- truly model all I believe about teaching and learning."

In my own observations and reflections, I have seen two consistent qualities to which I can aspire. People who are effective in their advocacy develop strong relationships and know when to push against established limitations.

Lesson Number 2: Build Allies

Twenty-two teachers, several coaches and administrators sit in a circle toward the end of a week of training to be coaches for Critical Friends Groups in their schools and districts. As the days passed, a sense of community has emerged and the conversations about teaching and learning have deepened. Everyone is open about the challenges and sincere in efforts to help one another with ideas and ways to think about solutions to sticky problems. They are about to begin creating action plans. We keep hearing about an underlying concern that when they return to their settings, they will inevitably face resistance and systemic constraints. It is not an ideal world. I worry about this. How can they work through all these challenges? They ask, "When this or that happens, what do you do?" The answers to these questions are never simple because each situation contains its own combination of variables. The facilitators respond with options and guiding questions. However, there is one consistent principle within every answer; without attention to relationships, none of the options will succeed.

Gather others around you who share your sense of purpose. Consider not only how others may join you in your purpose but also how you can join them. Look at the bigger picture of what's good for everyone. This could mean volunteering to serve on district committees or showing how you are a contributing force in the larger context—district, state, and so on.

Listen. Let people see you are really listening to both positive and negative opinions. Listen for what is underlying negative comments. Get to the real issues. Be glad if people come to you with their anger instead of talking where you can't address it. Seek them out and give them opportunities to participate and be heard.

Lots of people will get in your way. Move on from them to the ones who can help you. Tell them what you are trying to do and ask them how they can help you. Find a way to be on the same road.

Who can support you? What are these individuals trying to accomplish? How could you work with them toward common goals? Look at the dynamics of power in your setting and think about what would happen if there was a shift in perception. What if the administration, districts, school boards, or departments of education were posed not as enemies but as part of a dynamic and logical interaction? What if you gave the same respect and appreciation to the system as you do to an individual teacher/administrator or child whom you see as friendly to your cause? What if you were to look for the strengths and worth of the system on its own terms? What if you believed that everyone is working toward the same goal and common cause?

Don't wait for other people (especially those in authority) to set the tone or level of friendliness—reach out to make it what you want it to be. Having worked with people in various administrative positions, I have come to realize that many of them spend their time and considerable energy developing structures and systems to support effective teaching. Build allies at any level in the system to which you have access. Help them to work at the next levels they can reach. I have experienced times when the team of outside staff developers, teachers, and administrators working with the support of the district administrators has led to improved teaching and learning. Just as with students and teachers, it is crucial to see the system as composed of individuals rather than a monolithic bloc.

Use the same principles of establishing relationships to build allies among individuals and groups in the larger community—parents, police and fire personnel, senior citizens, and so forth.

Lesson Number 3: Practice Fearlessness

The prerequisite to change is often discomfort. The willingness to risk being the impetus for that discomfort—the one who points out the need for change—takes courage and an authentic appreciation of the value of learning and growth. We might well welcome agitation as a sign that progress is close at hand. As Frederick Douglass, the abolitionist leader and orator, explained:

> Power concedes nothing without a demand.
> It never has, and it never will.
> If there is no struggle, there is no progress.
> Those who profess to favor freedom, and yet deprecate agitation are men who want crops without plowing the ground.
> They want rain without thunder and lightning.
> They want the ocean without the awful roar of its waters.

Accepting that difficulty does not equal wrong is a crucial element of the journey, as the hero inevitably encounters troubles along the way to the destination.

Sometimes people appreciate the agitator who helps them face issues and take actions that might be long overdue. In *A Mythic Life* (1996), Jean Houston recalls what she learned from Margaret Mead: "It was important to challenge people at odd moments and in unlikely situations. That, she said, would throw them off base and get them moving and thinking again." When there is not consensus about valid evidence for what works and, therefore, no authentic united momentum in one direction, continue to bring the question to the surface and maintain the conversation.

Look for and lean on opportunities when they arise. The story of the teachers at Foster Elementary School provides many examples of individuals who were willing to challenge the status quo. Marcia Hecox's push for an inclusion model; Pauline Bustamante's recognition that a new principal would bring the school community to its next step, even though they were quite content with her; Ellin Keene's insistence on pointing out the teachers' own resistance to reading difficult material. In their study groups, they pushed themselves with difficult, challenging choices of texts to read.

Lesson Number 4: This Is a Personal Journey

Joy Hood tells a story about when she was a principal faced with an unpleasant personnel decision on which she had to take action. A friend told her, "Be the person you want to be even when you are doing something you don't want to do." Rather than being drawn into distracting battles, she held that counsel and maintained her sense of purpose.

In *The Courage to Teach* (1998), Parker J. Palmer argues that good teaching stems not from methods and techniques but from the person's identity and integrity as a teacher. We teach who we are. He provides a suggestion to help teachers get beneath their knowledge of methods to identify with the good teacher inside. He offers a sentence to complete: "When I am at my best as a teacher, I am like a _____." Ask yourself how you can be a hero as a teacher. Or choose another metaphor that helps you hold onto what you believe about yourself and your work.

Charles Handy, a British writer and consultant on organizational and management issues, writes that in our work lives some of us are elephants—moving steadily up the hierarchy to positions of weighty power—while others are fleas, that is, small and quick, living on the edges, and continually bothering the elephant to keep him moving. Both are needed and both need each other. I often use the metaphor of myself as a flea living at the margins and nipping at the elephant, perhaps causing a stampede. This image has also given me comic relief to offset discouragement.

Historian Taylor Branch (2002) says that during the Civil Rights movement, the Freedom Fighters saw themselves every day as founding fathers. This gave them the vision of a positive outcome and an inner sense of creation that helped them push beyond everyday limits. He suggests an exercise in establishing a courageous identity. Choose what has been a boundary in the past and take a step across it to stretch yourself beyond your habits. It's about who you are and what you do.

Powerful leaders and advocates use their heads, hearts, and hands. Using each of these aspects of ourselves makes it possible to simultaneously and effectively build allies and practice fearlessness. Think literally of your head, heart, and hand before going into a new situation. What are you thinking? What are you feeling? And finally, what will you do?

What Story Will You Tell?

While the gusts of change may seem to be blowing against us, Kate Hitzke, a friend from Australia, reminds me that in her country, "a very small seed and a strong wind get into the bloodiest places." With the opportunities provided by the steps and frameworks described in this book—teachers, administrators, and staff developers joined in a united effort to identify and establish effective meaningful teaching for all students—we collect seed ideas to step across the boundary and continue living a story of ongoing, practical professional learning based on a body of knowledge and success in teaching and learning.

The seeds of this story are already in the wind and, in some places, even planted. It has taken us time to catch up to the changes in the world. Now we can say here is what we know. Here is what we can do. This is our life, our work, our profession. Here is what we will continue to learn.

Though a good story is supposed to have a beginning, middle, and end, this story about continual learning might not have a proper ending. Those five young teachers each chose a different option that took them in different and yet similar directions. Three stayed at the school. Two went to another school. All five of these women encountered new challenges the following years but they did not alter their central commitment to continue with what they could do best for the children. As teacher Sandy Selzer said to me in reflecting on her own experiences, "We can affect change. The common language and strategy instruction is still strong. Our work and commitment has lived because we as teachers continue to model using it."

What did change for the five teachers was their belief in the scope of their responsibility as advocates for children's welfare in the whole school as well as in the classroom. They became more politically savvy in building relationships and judging when to take risks to speak out for what they believed was right. They learned to watch the forces around them outside of their classrooms. They sought opportunities to articulate their vision, show evidence of progress, and build trust between themselves and the people who could exert power over them and their school's destiny.

Still, the tug they feel most strongly is toward the work in their own classrooms. They know that eventually it all comes down to each individual child and adult—the impact of each teacher on student achievement. When we affect the children and the schools, we affect the larger situation.

With images of the faces, sounds of the voices, and the diverse and similar stories of those children and adults I see in schools every day, I continue to imagine this story. If we keep getting up and going to school, taking another step, each day we will learn something more about how to do a better job. If we maintain the effort to provide exemplary education for every child, we will continue to create schools as expanding worlds of learning. What a story that will be.

A final thought from T. H. White in *The Once and Future King* (1958), a classic hero's journey:

"The best thing for being sad," replied Merlin . . . "is to learn something. That is the only thing that never fails. You may grow old and trembling in your anatomies, you may lie awake at night listening to the disorder of your veins, . . . you may see the world around you devastated by evil lunatics, or know your honor trampled in the sewers of baser minds. There is only one thing for it then—to learn. Learn why the world wags and what wags it. That is the only thing which the mind can never exhaust, never alienate, never be tortured by, never fear or distrust, and never dream of regretting. Learning is the thing for you."

References

Barth, Roland. 2001. *Learning by Heart*. San Francisco: Jossey-Bass.

Branch, Taylor. 2002. Transcript of Closing Keynote Address. Public Education Network Conference. Washington, DC.

Campbell, Joseph. 1972. *The Hero with a Thousand Faces*. Princeton, NJ: Princeton University Press.

Campbell, Linda, Bruce Campbell, and Dee Dickinson. 1998. *Teaching and Learning Through Multiple Intelligences*. Boston: Allyn & Bacon.

Capote, Truman. 1975. *Music for Chameleons*. New York: Vintage Books.

Carini, Louis. 2000. *Spiritual Humanism*. Philadelphia: Xlibrio.

Carini, Patricia F. 1986. "Building from Children's Strengths." *Journal of Education* 168(3): 14–24.

Colorado Critical Friends Group. 2002. Coaches. Working Together to Improve Student Learning: Summer Seminar Resource Notebook. Denver, CO: CCFG.

Cook, Cathy. 1997. Critical Issue: Evaluating Professional Development. North Central Regional Educational Laboratory. Available at: www.ncrel.org/sdrs/areas/issues/educatrs/profdev/pd500.htm.

Danielson, Charlotte. 1996. *Enhancing Professional Practice: A Framework for Teaching*. Alexandria, VA: ASCD.

Darling-Hammond, Linda. 1998. "Restructuring Brief: A Publication of the California Professional Development Consortia," no. 15. Sacramento, CA: California Department of Education.

Deal, Terrence, and Kent Peterson. 1995. *The Leadership Paradox*. San Francisco: Jossey-Bass.

Fielding, Linda, and P. David Pearson. 1994. "Reading Comprehension: What Works?" *Educational Leadership* 51(5): 62–67.

Froebel, Frederick. 1974. *Education of Man*. Clifton, NJ: Augustus M. Kelley.

Fullan, Michael, and Andy Hargreaves. 1997. *What's Worth Fighting for in the Principalship?* New York: Teachers College Press.

Fullan, Michael G. 1993. *Change Forces: Probing the Depths of Educational Reform*. London: Falmer Press.

———. 1999. *Change Forces: The Sequel*. London: Falmer Press.

Garmston, Robert. 1997. *The Presenter's Fieldbook: A Practical Guide*. Norwood, MA: Christopher-Gordon.

Garmston, Robert, and Bruce Wellman. 1998. "Teacher Talk That Makes a Difference." *Educational Leadership* 55(7): 30–38.

Glasser, William, M.D. 1998. *The Quality School: Managing Students Without Coercion*. New York: Harper Perennial.

Harvey, Stephanie. 1998. *Nonfiction Matters: Reading, Writing, and Research in Grades 3–8*. Portland, ME: Stenhouse.

Harvey, Stephanie, and Anne Goudvis. 2000. *Strategies That Work: Teaching Comprehension to Enhance Understanding*. Portland, ME: Stenhouse.

Harwood, A. C. 1981. *The Recovery of Man in Childhood*. Herndon, VA: Anthroposophic.

Heifitz, Ronald. 1994. *Leadership Without Easy Answers*. Cambridge, MA: Belknap Press.

Horton, Myles. 1998. *The Long Haul: An Autobiography*. New York: Teachers College Press.

Houston, Jean. 1996. *A Mythic Life*. New York: Harper-Collins.

Jensen, Eric. 1998. *Teaching with the Brain in Mind*. Alexandria, VA: Association for Supervision and Curriculum Development.

Keene, Ellin Oliver, and Susan Zimmermann. 1997. *Mosaic of Thought: Teaching Comprehension in a Reader's Workshop*. Portsmouth, NH: Heinemann.

Lambert, Linda. 1998a. "Building Leadership Capacity." *Educational Leadership* 55(7): 17–20.

———.1998b. *Building Leadership Capacity in Schools*. Alexandria, VA: ASCD.

Lewis, Anne C. 1997. "A New Consensus Emerges on the Characteristics of Good Professional Development." *Harvard Education Letter* 13(May/June):1–4.

Lopez, Barry. 1990. *Crow and Weasel*. New York: North Point Press.

Lowry, Judith. 1999. *Gardening with a Wild Heart*. Berkeley, CA: University of California Press.

Meier, Deborah. 1995. *The Power of Their Ideas: Lessons for America from a Small School in Harlem*. Boston: Beacon Press.

———. 2002. *In Schools We Trust: Creating Communities of Learning in an Era of Testing and Standardization*. Boston: Beacon Press.

Miller, Debbie. 2002. *Reading with Meaning: Teaching Comprehension in the Primary Grades*. Portland, ME: Stenhouse.

Montessori, Maria. 1994. *For My Teacher*. Compiled by Suzanne Siegel Zenkel. White Plains, NY: Peter Pauper Press.

Moore, Thomas. 1996. *The Reenchantment of Everyday Life*. New York: HarperCollins.

Moss, Steve. 1998. *The World's Shortest Stories: Murder, Love, Horror, Suspense, All This and Much More in the Most Amazing Short Stories Ever Written, Each One Just 55 Words Long*. Philadelphia, PA: Running Press.

National Commission on Teaching and America's Future. 1996. *What Matters Most: Teaching for America's Future*. New York: National Commission on Teaching and America's Future.

National School Reform Faculty. 2003. Available at *www.harmonyschool.org*.

Palmer, Parker J. 1998. *The Courage to Teach*. San Francisco: Jossey-Bass.

Payne, Ruby. 2001. *A Framework for Understanding Poverty*. Highlands, TX: aha! Process, Inc.

Pearson, Carol S. 1986. *The Hero Within*. San Francisco: HarperCollins.

Pearson, P. David, Jan Dole, G. G. Duffy, and L. R. Roehler. 1992. "Developing Expertise in Reading Comprehension: What Should Be Taught and How Should It Be Taught?" In *What Research Has to Say to the Teacher of Reading*. 2d ed. Edited by J. Fartstup and S. J. Samuels. Newark, DE: International Reading Association.

Perkins, David. 1992. *Smart Schools: Better Thinking and Learning for Every Child*. New York: Free Press.

Prospect's Descriptive Processes: The Child, the Art of Teaching, the Classroom and School. The Prospect Archive and Center for Education and Research. Available from *www.prospectcenter.org*.

Puzo, Mario. 1964. *The Fortunate Pilgrim.* New York: Random House.

Raban, Jonathan. 1996. *Bad Land: An American Romance.* New York: Vintage Books.

Ray, Katie Wood. 1999. *Wondrous Words: Writers and Writing in the Elementary Classroom.* Urbana, IL: National Council of Teachers of English.

Ritchart, Ron. 2002. *Intellectual Character: What It Is, Why It Matters and How to Get It.* San Francisco: Jossey-Bass.

Robb, Laura. 2000. *Redefining Staff Development: A Collaborative Model for Teachers and Administrators.* Portsmouth, NH: Heinemann.

Sparks, Dennis. 1994. "A Paradigm Shift in Staff Development." *Journal of Staff Development.* 15 (Fall).

Sparks, Dennis, and Susan Loucks-Horsley. 1990. "Five Models of Staff Development for Teachers." Oxford, OH: National Staff Development Council.

Stefanakis, Evangeline. 2002. *Multiple Intelligences and Portfolios: A Window Into the Learner's Mind.* Portsmouth, NH: Heinemann.

Sweeney, Diane. 2003. *Learning Along the Way: Professional Development By and for Teachers.* Portland, ME: Stenhouse.

Sweet, Anne P., Richard W. Riley, Sharon P. Robinson, and Joseph C. Conaty. 1993. *State of the Art: Transforming Ideas for Teaching and Learning to Read.* Washington DC: OERI.

Tovani, Cris. 2000. *I Read It but I Don't Get It: Comprehension Strategies for Adolescent Readers.* Portland, ME: Stenhouse.

Trungpa, Chögyam. 1988. *Shambhala: The Sacred Path of the Warrior.* Boston: Shambhala Publications.

White, T. H. 1958. *The Once and Future King.* New York: Putnam.

Wright, Courtni C. 1994. *Journey to Freedom: A Story of the Underground Railroad.* New York: Holiday House.

Zemelman, Steven, Harvey Daniels, and Arthur Hyde. 1998. *Best Practice: New Standards for Teaching and Learning in America's Schools.* 2d ed. Portsmouth, NH: Heinemann.